Mothers,
Mystics
AND Merrymakers

Mothers, Mystics
and Merrymakers

Medieval Women Pilgrims

SARAH HOPPER

SUTTON PUBLISHING

First published in the United Kingdom in 2006 by
Sutton Publishing Limited · Phoenix Mill
Thrupp · Stroud · Gloucestershire · GL5 2BU

British Library Cataloguing in Publication Data
A catalogue record for this book is available from the British Library.

ISBN 0-7509-3800-5

Typeset in 11/14.5pt Sabon.
Typesetting and origination by
Sutton Publishing Limited.
Printed and bound in England by
J.H. Haynes & Co. Ltd, Sparkford.

To dear Miriam
(30 November 1972– 7 July 2005),
with love and many happy memories

A good wif was there of biside Bath . . .
And thries hadde she been at Jerusalem.
She hadde passed many a straunge foreign strem;
At Rome she hadde been, and at Boloigne,
In Galice at Seint-James, and at Coloigne.
She koude muchel of wandrynge by the weye.

Geoffrey Chaucer: *General Prologue to the*
Canterbury Tales, ll. 445–67

Contents

Acknowledgements

I would like to thank again those specialists and archivists who have given of their time and expertise so generously in the course of my research. Their guidance and encouragement have been the source of much inspiration. My thanks also to the readers who have cast their discerning eye over the manuscript and to the inspired team at Sutton Publishing for their skilled and professional approach.

To Dr Diana Webb at King's College, London, I would like to extend particular thanks, for support as well as for her translations of some of the original source material.

Finally, I wish to acknowledge the enthusiasm and support of my husband, mother, family, friends, and the encouragement of a special, sadly departed friend in whose memory this book is lovingly dedicated.

Introduction

All those which be at Rome knowe well that the women there be passing desirous to goo on pilgrimage and to touch and kiss every holy relik . . .[1]

The aim of this book is to highlight some of the many roles played and influences exerted by women in the practice of medieval pilgrimage and the vast industry that grew up around it. Few in number by comparison with their male counterparts, the medieval woman's pilgrimage experience was often unique and the few surviving accounts offer intriguing insights into what it really meant to be a woman embarking on such a journey, whether to a local shrine or on a more adventurous journey overseas. The motives of such women were often greatly determined by their duties as homemakers and child-bearers, roles which in turn influenced the kind of shrines they visited and the saints whom they petitioned. Their accounts of the dangers they faced and of their religious experiences offer valuable insights into medieval women's beliefs, expectations and aspirations, as well as into the nature of the society of which they were part.

I have chosen specific areas of enquiry that seem best to define the most significant aspects of medieval women's pilgrimage. Needless to say, any one of these topics easily constitutes a field of study in its own right. This work, therefore, seeks to offer a springboard for further research into any of the topics covered. These include an overview of the social classes of the women who undertook these journeys – from the most lowly to queens and empresses, from nuns and anchoresses to ordinary wives and mothers; a discussion of their means and motives; an analysis of the experiences they report and of the dangers and receptions they encounter; as well as a look at how women pilgrims were perceived by their male counterparts, contemporary commentators and in narrative fiction. The book concludes with an assessment of the vociferous opposition encountered by women pilgrims, criticism that began as early as the fourth century with concerns expressed for their safety and reached its most strident and threatening form in the fourteenth and fifteenth centuries. In the course of my discussion I shall introduce some of the most illuminating source material, as well as present both real and fictional female protagonists.

First and foremost, however, it is important to consider the position of such women within the everyday fabric of medieval society. There are several different, usually stereotypical, portrayals of such women in contemporary art and literature, from their depiction on misericord carvings as gossips in church (thus enticing the devil to take up residence in their horned headdresses), as witches and husband beaters, to their roles as homemakers, mothers and wives (the property of their husbands), and as both victims and perpetrators of domestic violence. Contemporary literature was often heavily misogynistic, describing women as incapable of remaining faithful to their husbands and lacking in dignity and self-control. Those who were particularly attractive might find their looks a mixed blessing and, were considered the most likely to stray and sacrifice their honour.

Chaucer describes the Wife of Bath's fifth husband as engrossed in his book of 'wikked wives', a text which recounts those women who through cunning and betrayal bring about the deaths of their poor husbands, luckless men who have nails driven into their skulls, are murdered or brought to ruin. Chaucer took his anti-female invective from two Roman sources, the epistle of Valerius on not taking a wife and that on the state of marriage by Theophrastus (a friend of Aristotle) and expounded several of their themes in his Wife of Bath's Prologue and Tale.

When viewed against the backdrop of such predominantly negative portrayals of women, we begin to appreciate that their freedom of movement could sometimes be restricted, if not by the Church then by their husbands or male kin. Certainly, as early as the fourth century, women pilgrims who travelled abroad were already raising a few eyebrows. Concerns were voiced at the dangers posed to their chastity and modesty outside their familiar environment. The women themselves had a whole host of reasons for wishing to embark on such journeys, including pilgrimages for the sake of sick or deceased husbands or, crucially, as wives and mothers to pray for the safekeeping and longevity of their families. Medieval women pilgrims played an important role in the practice of pilgrimage; the manner and type of journeys they undertook may be seen as extensions of their roles within the family and home. Of course, some were engaged in a quest for spiritual fulfilment; some chose never to return; others sought to embrace the religious life permanently, becoming anchoresses, joining nunneries or remaining in a continuous state of pilgrimage. And for others still, the journey could be undertaken for less noble reasons – in pursuit of personal gratification, or to serve as a means of diversion or escape. It could, too, be the occasion for revelry with pious pilgrimage merely a pretext. All of the above forms the subject of this book.

Durham

Ripon

York Beverley

Holywell

Walsingham
Bromholme

Ely

Worcester
Hereford
Hailes
Gloucester Winchcombe

LONDON

Rochester Canterbury

Salisbury
Shaftesbury Winchester
Whitchurch

St. Michael's Mount

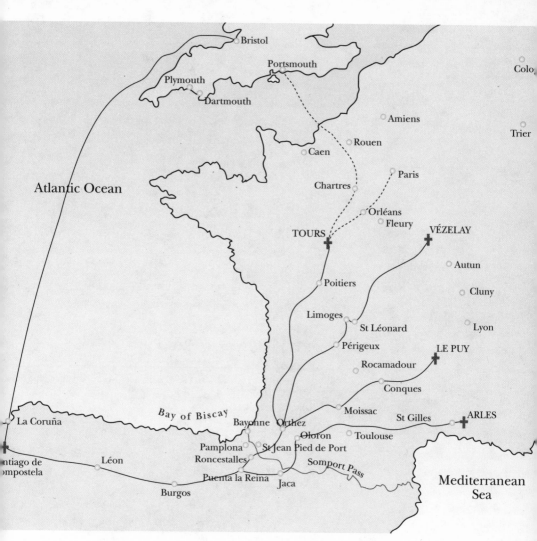

A map of the routes to Santiago de Compostela in northern Spain. *(Sarah Hopper)*

Opposite: A map showing some of the important English shrines. *(Sarah Hopper)*

xvii

ONE

Women on Pilgrimage – Reasons and Motivation

My mother behested another image of wax of the weight of you to our Lady of Walsingham . . . and I have behested to go on pilgrimage to Walsingham and Saint Leonard's for you. . . . I had never so heavy a season as I had fro the time that I wost of your sickness.[1]

In a fourteenth-century behavioral handbook for women, three things are highlighted as reasons that might drive a man away from his home: 'a quarrelsome wife, a smoking fireplace and a leaking roof . . .'.[2] A century earlier, in a guide for anchoresses (women who chose to forsake society for a life of asceticism and seclusion), we note that women too might have had good cause to want to escape the home: 'The wife stands, her child screams, the cat is at the flitch and the hound at the hide. Her cake is burning on the stove and her calf is suckling all the milk up; the pot is running into the fire and the churl is scolding.'[3]

1

This deliberately bleak portrayal of the medieval housewife's existence is in fact highly plausible. Medieval women existed in a society in which everything – from religion and home life, to work, the arts and literature – was controlled by men. Once married, their possessions and free will became those of their husbands; it is only in misogynistic literature that women appear who achieve 'sovreigntee' over their husbands, something they usually acquired by treacherous or underhand means. Often drawing on earlier texts concerning the state of marriage, certain misogynistic ideas were current that presented women as incapable of controlling their own behaviour, their minds or even their tongues when it came to preserving their honour. Thus it was deemed safest for the 'fragile sex' to remain under the direction of their husbands and fulfil their role within the home.

Perhaps it is no surprise that there were some medieval women who sought freedom or independence, even to escape the confines of such a constrained existence and who might therefore grasp the opportunity to journey on pilgrimage, a practice endorsed by the Church; at the very least it was a diversion from their everyday realities, an idea reflected in contemporary literature. For example, while drawing on early sources to highlight the pitfalls of marriage, the Prologue and Tale of Chaucer's Wife of Bath, one of the best-known and widely travelled women pilgrims, abounds in images of female power and 'sovreigntee' in the home exercised by wives over their husbands (of which she herself has had five). In a world driven by men and male power, the Wife of Bath finds her freedom by becoming a perpetual pilgrim. Of course, men too may have wished for some diversion from the daily hardships and responsibilities of medieval life, although their roles and status usually afforded them greater latitude than their womenfolk in this respect.

There is evidence to suggest that women might also have embarked on pilgrimage as a form of refuge, as in the case of one woman whose son had drowned. Having been the first to find him, she subsequently went on pilgrimage, undoubtedly in part to pray for his soul and commend him to God's safekeeping. However, instead of choosing a local shrine, she takes herself off on an ambitious journey to the Holy Land, during which she too sadly dies.[4]

While many pilgrims had never left the environs of their own villages before embarking on pilgrimage, women had even less opportunity to travel or venture outside their home patch. They might also, it is true, find themselves away from home, in the undesirable role of social outcast, harlot or wanderer, all of which roles cast them in an unenviable light. All occupations involving travel such as that of messenger, minstrel, trader, peddler and merchant were confined to men.

For practical as well as incidental reasons, the majority of women would have undertaken pilgrimages only to local shrines rather than set out on journeys that took them away from the home for long periods. In the case of Chaucer's Prioress, for example, it is fair to assume that her modest, domestic pilgrimage was of a kind more common among womenfolk and nuns in particular, although Chaucer placed her outside the cloister in the first place for deliberate effect. Much might also depend on circumstance, or whether a vow or the terms of a will enjoined travel to a specific shrine. This is not to suggest that women of a more lowly class did not make the more arduous journeys overseas, however. The Wife of Bath has openly forsaken domestic and familial ties, instead her state of perpetual pilgrimage accounts for her impressive itinerary which covers visits to Rome, Jerusalem, Santiago de Compostela and Cologne.

The Wife's pilgrimage includes those holy destinations then at the height of favour and sacred prestige. From the fourth-century departure for the Holy Land in the time of Paula and Egeria, to the increasing popularity of Rome from the eighth and ninth centuries for its associations with Christ's apostles, and the legendary rediscovery of the body of St James in Spain in the ninth, these three pilgrimage destinations were to enjoy enduring acclaim. The Holy Land was ever popular as the home of Jesus, where pilgrims

3

were able literally to follow in His footsteps and revisit the settings of His life and Passion as they were described in the Bible. As the seat of the Roman Catholic Church, Rome was particularly important and Santiago de Compostela, where legend had it that St James was buried, offered the pilgrim its own spectacular cathedral in north-west Spain. There were, too, a host of other saints' shrines scattered liberally across Europe; some were situated on the pilgrim routes that led to these three sacred centres, and others drew equal acclaim and veneration, such as that of Canterbury. Aside from the smaller, more accessible local shrines that were perhaps better suited to the medieval woman's routine, whether as mother or widow, just as their male counterparts, women pilgrims would also weather the arduous journeys that led to the most famous sites of pilgrimage.

While there were no laws preventing women from travelling away from home, only loud dissent from certain quarters and misogynistic invective, criticism usually focused on the widespread medieval perception of the female's inherent mental and physical weakness. For both wife and husband, however, it was necessary for a statement of consent to be granted each to the other if either of them wished to leave home on pilgrimage. In the case of Margery Kempe, who left behind a spouse, business and several children, her husband eventually granted her request after an epoch of denied sexual relations from his newly chaste wife, who was suddenly driven to set out on a spiritual quest to those most prominent shrines. Her husband accompanied her on some of her early journeys to English shrines; later he gave his consent for her journeys abroad when she explained that Christ commanded that she visit Rome, Jerusalem and Santiago de Compostela. However, when Margery falls out of favour with her hosts, they challenge her right to go on pilgrimage without her husband. She is asked if she has a letter giving her husband's permission, to which she replies that he had given her his verbal consent.

The paucity of written records makes it impossible to put an accurate figure on the numbers of medieval women pilgrims, forcing us instead to discuss their participation in more general terms. Occasionally, women pilgrims' activities and demeanour are recorded by their companions, offering tantalising insights; sometimes, such records imply the complete absence of women in a pilgrimage party. In the accounts of Brother Felix Fabri's journeys to the Holy Land, he more than once makes a point of naming individually each pilgrim in the parties among whom he finds himself, all of them men. This is telling, but not surprising. Yet elsewhere in Fabri's accounts he also offers valid insights into the experiences of the few women whom he does encounter as fellow pilgrims along the way.

Of particular interest to our discussion is Diana Webb's detailed study of the pilgrimage activity of one Italian city, Pistoia, in which she notes that between 1360 and 1460 some 3,000 pilgrims are recorded in the office of works of the city's patron, St James. Not all of these are named, but among them are 200 or so women who include those of lowly rank, a laundress and a cook. Also highlighted is the fact that the majority of these women took their journeys before 1400 rather than after. This 'cut off' date will be examined more fully in Chapter 12, 'Pilgrimage under Fire', which discusses contemporary opposition to pilgrimage, in particular as it affected women.[5]

The surviving chronicles of women pilgrims are few, particularly in comparison with those of their male contemporaries. The fifteenth-century, dictated account of Margery Kempe is probably our most accessible and candid picture of the experience of a woman pilgrim. However, along with those letters of her earlier Roman and Anglo-Saxon counterparts, such as Paula and the Abbess Eadburga, Chaucer's rendering of women pilgrims in his *Canterbury Tales*, as well as surviving wills, letters, legal papers and other documents, there is sufficient evidence to arrive at a reasonably informed appreciation of what it meant to be a woman on medieval pilgrimage and to highlight the unique nature of their experience as travellers outside their accustomed, domestic milieu.

In his letter to the Archbishop of Canterbury in AD 747, St Boniface distinguished two categories of contemporary women pilgrims, matrons (widows) and veiled women, those of holy orders. Undoubtedly, among these were women also seeking empowerment and escape, adventure and merriment. For those women from religious orders, however, there is evidence that they had to strive harder than most to obtain consent for their journeys. Conversely, men in holy orders bent on pilgrimage were a familiar sight in medieval England, as were wandering friars and those travelling in the performance of papal and religious duties. While a nun would be required to seek approval through similar channels as a monk, she often met with greater opposition to her request on the grounds of potential dangers and threats to her modesty.

It was argued, too, that nuns did not need to undertake pilgrimage to holy shrines in order to recommend themselves to God, for they had already dedicated themselves to His service within the cloister. While the Abbess of Minster in Thanet, Kent, managed to obtain special dispensation from Pope Boniface VIII to leave her house to go on pilgrimage, it was believed that the duties of the cloistered nun lay essentially within the convent. Earlier in the same century, Pope Boniface had abstained from offering the Abbess Eadburga advice either for or against her request to make pilgrimage to Rome, although he was later honest enough to admit that 'our sister Wiethburga' had benefited from inner peace and tranquillity as a result of her visit to the shrine of St Peter. (Not only did Eadburga conduct her pilgrimage to Rome but she met Boniface there in the middle of the eighth century.)

Female mystics used pilgrimage travel to overcome the rigid gender boundaries of the time and to educate themselves while on the road. The conventionally pious and indomitably devout Margery Kempe left behind a husband, failed brewery business and several children in King's Lynn, Norfolk, to seek spiritual learning and salvation through pilgrimage. Many more were undertaking pilgrimage on behalf of their husbands, children and families to request divine help in childbearing and the health or preservation of their offspring. Familial concerns continued to be an overriding incentive for women undertaking pilgrimage. Female fertility, for example, was taken to be a gift from God, while inability to conceive was a curse, perhaps due to the weight of one's sin or unabsolved transgressions, and such issues would be brought to appropriate shrines for the intercession of specifically invoked saints. Problems with conception might also be interpreted as the result of adultery, for which the woman had been punished with barrenness, or were even believed to be a consequence of their having been married without observing the conventions of fidelity and obedience to her husband. Failure to conceive was also something that brought hopeful fathers-to-be to pilgrim shrines, especially kings hoping to produce strong heirs. Among their number was Henry VIII in the sixteenth century and the King of Poland in the twelfth; the latter eventually sent several gifts and a small model of a baby boy made of gold to the shrine of St Gilles in Provence, before his baby son was conceived and born.

 Pilgrimage was endorsed and prescribed by the Church as a way of repairing the moral order of one's life as well as of commending one's soul to God, a significant factor in making a request for divine intervention in such matters as conception and bearing children. Several miracle stories conclude with the forgiveness of the subject's sin before the miraculous healing or intervention can occur. Sometimes the subject is even told by the saint to leave their shrine and return only once they have amended their lives and their sins have been absolved.

Documentary evidence also suggests that some children accompanied their mothers and endured the rigours of pilgrimage. The orders written by Roger de Moulins in 1181 for the hospital of St John in Jerusalem reveal that some women also undertook pilgrimage while they were pregnant. His directives make provision for mothers who gave birth in the hospital by supplying cradles for their newborn to prevent the 'overlaying' of babies.

In other instances, women set out with their offspring alongside them, such as in the case of Raimondo Palmario and his mother who sought permission from the Bishop of Piacenza to undergo pilgrimage to the Holy Sepulchre in Jerusalem. The bishop placed a red cross at each of their breasts as a symbol of their protection as pilgrims and blessed them on their way.[6] The Acta Sanctorum of St James relates the intriguing story of a mother who takes her crippled son to the relics of St James at the Basilica of St Zeno in Verona. She pushes him there in a cart on account of his humpback. In the church, witnesses watch as his bones begin to crack and his skin stretch as he takes on his new, re-formed body, before ably accompanying his mother back home to Florence on foot.

Just as with male pilgrims, women might have pilgrimage imposed on them by way of punishment or they might commit themselves to go on pilgrimage to fulfil an oath, often made in exchange for salvation from serious illness or in a moment of great danger. However, as we have seen the most common reasons for women to undertake pilgrimage relate to family members, often children, to pray for assistance in conceiving and at delivery and subsequently for the health and longevity of their offspring. Given their maternal and familial obligations, women were left with a defined if limited window of opportunity for undertaking longer, overseas travel. In her study of European pilgrimage, Diana Webb neatly encapsulates this decisive point, 'the segment of female lifespan available for large-scale pilgrimage was relatively limited. If child-bearing and the care of small children were past, health and energy must still suffice.'[7]

It is for these reasons that women often found themselves on pilgrimages either before conception, while pregnant (with or without their husbands) but thereafter usually not until they had raised their families, become widowed or were more advanced in years. These circumstances, however, did not prevent them from venturing to the more convenient local shrines. Here they prayed for help and there are many extant petitions relating to such smaller,

*familial +
domestic
commitments*

parochial shrines made by mothers of sick children or by those whose children have fallen victim to accidents such as drowning.[8]

It was the sheer weight of their familial and domestic commitments, which normally extended for the better part of their adult lives, that best explains medieval women's need to relinquish or receive dispensation from any pilgrimage vows. This was the case for Joanne de Pacy, who vowed with her husband to undertake a pilgrimage if she survived the traumatic birth of her baby. Later, her husband requested that her part of the vow be commuted as thereafter she was normally pregnant every year and so physically unable to make the journey. In another instance, in 1391, we find that a woman, having made a vow to her first husband that she would go on pilgrimage to Santiago, later remarried. However, her second husband refused consent for her to fulfil her vow to his predecessor. She therefore sought commutation of her vow on account of her several children and advanced years.

Later in life, widows might find themselves in possession of an inheritance or lands and, freed too from the better part of their domestic responsibilities, might go on pilgrimage for the benefit of the soul of their deceased spouse. Often, too, they found themselves able to make more extended journeys; some did not return, choosing instead to join a nunnery or opting for a life of seclusion as an anchoress. Brother Felix Fabri's account of his travels mentions a band of feisty, elderly widows who shared his sea passage to the Holy Land. Margery Kempe followed a similar pattern except that it was the money she inherited after the death of her wealthy father that allowed her to settle the family debts and depart on her own pilgrimage. An intrepid woman, she continued her travels into her sixties.

Those pilgrimages taken by wives in respect of a deceased spouse were either to carry out a pilgrimage vow that had been left unfulfilled by his death or, commonly, to pray for the safe passage of his soul to God. Such journeys are mostly recorded as having taken place about a year or so after the spouse's death, an interval which

9

allowed their affairs to be settled. For example, widow Alice de Bello Campo received protection to undertake such a journey 'beyond seas' in 1309. Likewise, Isolda Belhous, widow of John, had two letters, one from May 1330 affirming protection until Christmas to go to Santiago and a second for February the following year to go to Santiago until July, to which her husband had made a pilgrimage seventeen years earlier. Interestingly, it is frequently women who are requested to undertake pilgrimages on behalf of a testator. Given the poignancy of the moment at which such requests were made, it seems that women were considered the most reliable vessels for the carrying out of such wishes, in which fervent prayer for the soul of the deceased was a decisive part. In the case of male pilgrims or sons being appointed to such a duty through a will, the obligation to go on pilgrimage might be a condition of their entitlement to inherit.

Suffice it to say, women might equally find themselves left behind, keeping the home fires burning and running a business while their husbands were away on pilgrimage – indeed, this was another way in which wives might find themselves widowed, their husbands failing to return, having met with some fatal misadventure on the way. One Matilda, widow of William of Wolvesey, was requested to supply proof that her husband had actually died on pilgrimage before she was allowed to remarry. Fortunately, she was able to produce two witnesses who had been present at his death and burial.

Some women accompanied their husbands on pilgrimage, such as Alice and her husband Robert, son of Walter, who together set out for Jerusalem in 1310 having made provision for the livelihoods they were leaving behind through attorneys, to cover an absence of three years.

For the elderly or infirm, a 'proxy pilgrim' could be appointed to undertake the journey on their behalf. As with men, such instruction was sometimes written into a will to be carried out after their death. This was the case for Catherine of Aragon who requested that someone undertake pilgrimage to Walsingham. The purpose of such a pilgrimage was again for the sake of the subject's soul after death, particularly if it was a pilgrimage that they had vowed to make themselves in their lifetime, rendered unfulfilled by their illness or demise. This was the case for Margaret Est in 1484 who bequeathed money to Thomas Thurkeld to undertake this duty for her: 'and aft my disease he shall go unto seynt Thomas of Canterbury, and ther to prey for me to relesse me of my vowe whiche I made thirdyr myself . . .'.[9]

Such apparently valid and worthy motives aside, surviving evidence points to reservations concerning women taking pilgrimage that began to be voiced as early as the fourth century. In a letter to Archbishop Cuthbert of Canterbury in an attempt to discourage the tide of English female pilgrims to Rome, Pope Boniface wrote that 'a great part of them perish and few keep their virtue'. Similar opposition had gathered considerable momentum against male and female pilgrims collectively by the fourteenth century, when the Church and critics of pilgrimage were questioning its propriety and value when so many pilgrims seemed to stray from the spiritual path intended. For women, though, there was the added contention that their chastity and honour were dangerously imperilled by the experience of travel to foreign parts and that many were succumbing to this pitfall, willingly or otherwise. In the words of one commentator, there had come to be 'very few towns in Lombardy or Frankland or Gaul where there is not a courtesan or harlot of English stock'.[10]

While the concerns of Pope Boniface may often have been justified, there is contrary evidence to suggest that there were female pilgrims of good grace and ascetic piety, who experienced the impropriety of their male counterparts only as an obstacle of pilgrimage – Margery Kempe explains how she became disconcerted by 'indecent looks' from her male companions and feared for her chastity so that she 'dare not sleep any night'. The words of one Italian nobleman, seemingly with first-hand knowledge of such a scenario, would appear to endorse her concerns: 'How dangerous it is to lead young, nay attractive women (in whom levity and lust are inherent) into foreign parts . . . particularly inexperienced wives.'[11]

His words also articulate the established view that the 'fragile sex' were unable to control their own virtue and were therefore particularly vulnerable. Whether women's self-control or the inappropriate behaviour of their male counterparts was to blame, some thought it best to avoid putting themselves in such danger or temptation. By the fourteenth century, when the efficacy of pilgrimage had been subjected to closer scrutiny by the Church, Gregory of Tours had forbidden his three daughters to go on pilgrimage, and in a fourteenth-century handbook of manners and etiquette for women, Christine de Pisan likewise advised her fellow noble women against it, reasoning that pilgrimages were got up for no good reason and at a lot of needless expense.

With Pope Urban's council at Clermont and the decision to send an army of Christians to the Holy Land in 1095 to recover Jerusalem from the Saracens, some contemporary women had apparently found endorsement and the perfect excuse for their pilgrimage. It seems that several were as determined as their male counterparts to join those taking up the cross as *crucesignates* (crusaders) to recover Jerusalem and yet more intended to participate in Henry III's proposed pilgrimage in 1271. At that time, his daughter-in-law, Eleanor of Castile, accompanied her husband to Acre on this the Fifth Crusade (he would become King Edward I when Henry III died in 1272). Their daughter Joan of Acre would also take up the cross with her husband Gilbert de Clare, Earl of Gloucester, in July 1290. While the Church accepted that married women might accompany their husbands in this cause and even on occasion go without them, there were reservations about women's participation in the Crusades.

The main worry expressed was, again, that the women might lapse into immorality and even demoralise the fighting men, distracting them from the pious business in hand. And there was anxiety about the other side of the coin: crusades by the early fourteenth century posed a real threat to a woman's virtue in a land full of soldiers and mercenaries. A canon lawyer called Hostiensis was concerned about women joining the Crusades unless they were of good repute or advanced in years, presumably then strong-willed enough not to be swayed by temptation. In spite of these widely voiced reservations, detemined women did join Crusades. Among them were groups such as those led by Catherine of Siena, who in about 1374 sought permission from the Pope to make a pilgrimage to Jerusalem with her band of female followers and again in 1375 as a crusade against the Turks. She sought to achieve spiritual salvation by dying a martyr's death and she gained herself a significant female following both during her lifetime and after her death and later canonisation.

Brother Fabri highlighted the fourteenth-century enthusiasm for those enrolling as pilgrim crusaders:

> all men flocked together, urged by a most burning desire, from Spain, Provence, Aquitaine, Brittany, Scotland, England. . . . From all these countries men flocked and gathered together like lions who scent their prey . . . hermits and cloistered monks and maidens . . . and many nuns broke the bonds of their obedience without leave or licence, started forth from their cloister, and mingled with the ranks of armed men . . .[12]

Women undoubtedly played an important role as pilgrims and there is evidence that they did much to strengthen the popularity of certain shrines, saints' cults and to support the pilgrimage economy as a whole. There was also a host of female saints and figures of devotion in the medieval era towards whom much devotional energy was directed. Indeed, we must not forget that most cherished of all female figureheads, the Virgin Mary, who enjoyed a massive cult following in medieval England and one that subsequently came to boast its own 'Nazareth', in the shape of the Holy House at Walsingham, Norfolk.

TWO

The Widow, the Empress and the Nun – Early Women Pilgrims

A longing for God set on fire the heart of this most blessed nun Egeria. In the strength of the glorious Lord, she fearlessly set out on an immense journey to the other side of the world.[1]

Seventh-century letter of the Galician monk Valerius, encouraging his monks to emulate Egeria.

We are fortunate to have evidence for some of the earliest women pilgrims, some of whom elected to remain at their destinations, choosing never to return. Of those about whom most information exists, the most interesting are the fourth-century Spanish nun Egeria, the Roman matron Paula who went to live in Bethlehem, the Empress Helena, mother of Constantine who is alleged to have found the True Cross in AD 326, and St Bridget (Birgitta), who was especially venerated by medieval female pilgrims. The experiences of these early women pilgrims exerted a profound influence not only on the aspirations of the women who followed in their footsteps but also more generally in both secular and sacred writings. It is no coincidence that Chaucer has his Wife of Bath visit exactly the same sites in the Holy Land as did Paula.

While Pope Honorius had dismissed the efficacy of pilgrimage, claiming that it was mostly misused by those who 'gad about to holy places out of idle curiosity or a desire for human praise',[2] he nevertheless lavished praise on Helena, commending her generous donations to the poor and her genuinely ascetic impulse. Equally, in the fourth century St Jerome's letters had exalted the qualities of a Roman widow Paula and her virgin daughter Eustochium who went to live alongside him in Bethlehem. Their practices as early women pilgrims were endorsed by the highborn and powerful and set a precedent for those generations of women that followed.

Perhaps the most influential early woman pilgrim was the Empress Helena, her renown based on the discoveries she is said to have made in the Holy Land. These events served to establish an increasingly popular pilgrimage tradition to Jerusalem with specially designated sacred locations and the creation of a new, organised approach to the pilgrim experience there. In his 'Life of Constantine III', Eusebius described how four sacred sites had been concealed by a Roman temple on Hadrian's forum in the upper city, north of Mount Sion. Helena's son Constantine had ordered that the temple's pagan images, wood and stone be demolished and carried away. On removal of the earth, the Holy Sepulchre was exposed beneath the temple's ruins whereupon Constantine swiftly ordered that a Christian chapel be built to honour this sacred marvel.

It was Helena, however, who is recorded as having uncovered and identified the True Cross used for the Crucifixion, the most significant article of Christ's life and death and that which came to be the most prized among holy relics, sought after and aspired to by religious houses across Europe. Helena was said to have made her visit to the Holy Land at the age of eighty, in the year AD 326. In all, three crosses were uncovered but the True Cross was revealed through its perform-ance of a holy miracle. When laid over the body of a dead man, he was restored to life. This scene is depicted in the fresco of a tiny chapel of the Quatro Coronati in Rome, which can be viewed today.

'Saint Helena did not know for certain which was the cross Christ was killed on; so she took each one in turn and laid it on a dead man, and as soon as the True Cross was laid on the dead body, the corpse rose from death to life.'[3] The Empress Helena's high birth and influence doubtless played their part in the reverence and authenticity accorded her discovery, while her son Constantine's enterprise and resources facilitated the establishment of the holy sites as the original, biblical locations of Christ's Passion.

Helena's discovered cross became a highly revered holy relic almost immediately; having shown its miraculous power it was then taken to Constantinople whence it was brought to Rome. Today, a fragment of walnut wood housed in the Church of Sante Croce in Rome continues to fuel interest and speculation as to its authenticity. Kept close to another intriguing but no less unusual purported relic, the finger of Doubting Thomas, the wooden fragment is displayed as the original '*titulus*', or headboard of the True Cross of Christ's Crucifixion, derisively inscribed with the words, 'Jesus of Nazareth, King of the Jews' in Hebrew, Greek and Latin. We have rather more reason to believe that such a relic was being exhibited in Jerusalem at the time of the visit of another early woman pilgrim, the nun Egeria, in AD 380. It seems that the fragment was as revered in Egeria's time as it is today, by the curious and pious visitor alike. Egeria describes how it was brought out in a silver and gold reliquary and then the *titulus* and another fragment were laid on a table so that pilgrims might approach one by one and kiss the wood, until one pilgrim arrived who was particularly enthusiastic to take away his own souvenir: 'But on one occasion (I don't know when) one of them bit off a piece of the Holy Wood and stole it away, and for this reason the deacons stand round and keep watch in case anyone dares to do the same again.'[4]

The domed Church of the Holy Sepulchre was built on the Mount of Cavalry, Christianity's most sacred ground, where the Holy Cross was buried, also the alleged burial place of Christ and the site on which Christ's body was laid after the Crucifixion. Officially, those crucified were denied formal Jewish burial, but we are told that Joseph of Arimathea requested permission to bury Jesus's body. He placed it within a cave, the mouth of which was then sealed with a rock. Constantine applied his own private funds to the project, as well as state resources, ensuring that the Holy Sepulchre and its sacred contents bore enduring testimony to Christ's existence, thus permanently influencing the pilgrimage tradition to the Holy Land sites.

From the time of Helena's discovery in the early fourth century, the holy places of Jerusalem became the most revered of the pilgrimage sites. Set against the backdrop of Jesus's home terrain – the pilgrim could visit the places of his birth, life and death – the Holy Sepulchre now acted as a kind of memorial museum to the most poignant moments of His Passion, in accordance with scriptural teaching. The Anglo-Saxon pilgrim Saewulf noted a place within the walls of the Holy Sepulchre called 'compas', the spot from where God was said to have measured and marked out the centre of the world. The much later 1300 Mappa Mundi now in Hereford Cathedral significantly placed Jerusalem at the very heart of its cartographical world. In the late fourteenth century, the famous knight errant Sir John Mandeville was also to vocalise the significance of Jerusalem's Holy Sepulchre for the pilgrim: 'You must understand that when men arrive in Jerusalem, they make their first pilgrimage to the church where is the Sepulchre of our Lord.'[5]

One female pilgrim who wholeheartedly embraced the history and mapping out of the sacred sites of Jerusalem was the fourth-century Spanish nun Egeria. What survives of her contemporary correspondence points to her returning first from Mount Sinai to Jerusalem, having already spent over a year journeying between the sacred sites of the Holy Land, and then on to Constantinople to follow in the footsteps of Helena, and Christ. Egeria wrote informative letters back to her fellow nuns in Spain describing all that she saw in meticulous detail. It seems possible that she intended her sisters to be able to perform their own mental pilgrimage through the reading of her letters and by virtue of their comprehensive descriptions. She certainly imbued her writings with sufficient detail for an informed pilgrimage of the imagination, as well as describing different liturgical procedure there.

The *Travels* of Egeria had been lost for several hundred years, and when discovered, part of the account was missing. From what remains, one may surmise that she was travelling between AD 381 and AD 384 and that she had set out from the Atlantic coast, most likely Galicia. Her curiosity, eagerness and attention to detail make what survives of her writings a truly valuable modern resource for the study of fourth-century pilgrimage, for which nothing similar survives.

In a style reminiscent of St Jerome's lavish praise for Paula, a monk named Valerius commended the energy and fortitude of Egeria on her extensive travels, with the now familiar reference to women's surmounting of their inherent weaknesses. As with other later spirited women pilgrims, it was held that it was the strength of Egeria's faith that enabled her to conquer human and physical obstacles and overcome her inherent female weakness to be 'upheld by the right hand of God': 'her heart and her whole being were on fire with an earnest longing to seek the kingdom of heaven on high . . . so that she did not weary, and, even when she reached the summits of the most inaccessible mountains, the weakness of her body gave way, by God's help . . . she bore the effort lightly'.[6] Valerius even encourages his monks to view Egeria as an example: 'We cannot blush at this woman, dearest brothers. . . . While she sought healing for her own soul, she gave us an example of following God which is marvellously profitable for many . . . though we can scarcely deserve to merit God's grace in a measure equal to this exemplary woman, yet we have by our own choice promised to serve God faithfully in the religious life.'[7]

19

Egeria was one of the earliest pilgrims for whom we have documentary evidence, driven by a genuine religious fervour of the kind which the medieval Church considered became increasingly rare as the pilgrimage tradition continued over the centuries. Egeria truly believed in the efficacy of her journey and was deeply committed to viewing as many of the holy places as she could, as well as conveying her impressions and descriptions of them to her sisters as comprehensively as possible. At each site, Egeria requested the appropriate biblical passage be read out. Her writing is so dense, her descriptions so thorough that on the rare occasion that she is diverted, the reader is afforded a brief glimpse of her true personality, of the woman rather than of the nun and pilgrim scribe. For example, she briefly turns from her descriptions to relate how one day she had encountered an old friend on the way. 'I had come to know her in Jerusalem when she was up there on pilgrimage . . . and I simply cannot tell you how pleased we were to see each other again. But I must get back to the point . . .'

Egeria's journey was arduous, exacerbated by the usual discomforts and dangers of pilgrimage and to chance upon the familiar face of an old friend would indeed have been a comfort and a source of joy. Egeria clearly missed the nuns at her convent, affectionately terming them 'ladies of my heart' and 'loving ladies, light of my heart'. Unfortunately, however, her very focused style precludes any more penetrating analysis of Egeria's character or personality traits, although there is no disputing her genuinely ascetic and pious nature. Her style is also far less animated than that of, say, Margery Kempe in the fourteenth century, and she is far less inclined to speak about herself or her own emotional responses to the things she sees; nonetheless, from a modern perspective (and doubtless that of the sisters awaiting her letters in Spain) she does provide some very interesting details. For example, she relates how some pilgrims attempted to steal fragments of the wooden cross by biting bits off with their teeth. We know from a later, fourteenth-century account that it had also become common for pilgrims to steal away fragments of rock from the holy sites. Brother Fabri cites one pilgrim who had removed a piece from the Monastery of St Catherine of Sinai and warns pilgrims against stealing any rock from the Holy Sepulchre, saying that to do so was punishable by excommunication.

Egeria clearly had a drive and determination of spirit that pushed her on to visit many pilgrimage sites among the Holy Land's extensive repertoire. On more than one occasion, her letters suggest that she has reached the conclusion of her pilgrimage and will be returning home, only later to feel compelled to resume her travels to some further sacred sites. After her journey to Constantinople, in a final surviving instalment, Egeria writes that rather than return home, she now intends to visit other holy places in Asia Minor; and comments poignantly that she is unsure whether she will return home before she dies: 'My present plan is, in the name of Christ Our God to travel to Asia. . . . If after that I am still alive, and able to visit further places, I will either tell you about them face to face (if God so wills), or at any rate write to you about them if my plans change. In any case, ladies, light of my heart, whether I am "in the body" or "out of the body", please do not forget me.'[8] Egeria's ostensibly religious curiosity and enthusiasm ultimately transformed her pilgrimage into a state of perpetual, sacred journeying.

Roughly contemporaneous with Egeria's travels, letters survive that relate to the arrival of St Jerome in Bethlehem in AD 385, where he took up residence in neighbouring caves to those occupied by Paula and her daughter Eustochium. Jerome took a very academic and scholarly view of the sacred places among which he lived in the Holy Land and was normally not one to lavish praise on the numerous pilgrims who arrived to witness them for themselves while he was there. In fact he criticised their naïve belief that a transformation of their soul would occur merely through their presence in this holy environment. Paula, however, earned his admiration for her genuine piety and energy. In his Epistola

(CVIII/108) he recounts that he could barely believe the zeal and enthusiasm which his female companion exhibited as she quite 'forgot her sex and physical weakness!'

It would seem that the fourth century saw several such Roman women converted to Christianity and journeying to the Holy Land for the benefit of their souls, but only those surviving letters of Jerome and Paula survive. Paula's pilgrimage to the sacred places of the Holy Land was a re-creation of the life and Passion of Christ, her fervent responses triggered by what for her in particular were the highly charged sites within the Church of the Holy Sepulchre, or by gazing on a holy relic of Christ's Passion. So powerfully infused with emotion was Paula's mystical perception of the sacred sites that she relived each stage of the biblical drama with passion and conviction. This affective response to the holy places is something we witness again in the much later accounts of Margery Kempe.

Paula's first visit to the sites of the Passion was her most profound experience: 'She threw herself down in adoration before the cross as if she could see the Lord himself hanging from it. . . . What tears she shed there, what sighs of grief, all Jerusalem knows . . .'9 Similarly, when faced with the cave in which Christ was said to have been born, Paula believes that she sees before her, with the 'eyes of her soul', the infant Christ wrapped in swaddling clothes, crying in the manger. In fact, Paula shared her manner of experiencing the Holy Land with several other devout pilgrims before and after, in that she seems to have striven for a literal association of the physical with the spiritual state. This perhaps demonstrated a need inherent in the medieval psyche, as perhaps today, for something tangible to associate with the memory of a particular saint or holy figure – hence the immense popularity of relics, often said to be items that had actually belonged to the venerated figures and most often consisting of their earthly remains.

The opportunity to walk in Christ's footsteps was an understandably powerful experience for the medieval pilgrim, whose religious education would have consisted mostly of exposure to visual images and iconography, and to listening to passages from the Bible. The medieval imagination was finely tuned by comparison with our media exposed era and its response to visual stimuli pronounced. With this in mind it is not difficult to appreciate how relatively easily the pilgrim might be prompted to powerful imaginative re-creations of these iconic Christian scenes, such as the crucifixion or the nativity. The force of their experience also appears less outlandish in light of their very personal encounter with the sites of Christ's life and cruel death.

In his letters Jerome places great emphasis on the fact that Paula had been born into a wealthy and privileged family in Rome, affording her a luxurious lifestyle and high status. He describes how she used to dress in silks and was carried by eunuchs so that her feet might not touch the ground. We are told that she was descended from King Agamemnon and her husband from Aeneas. However, along with other high-born, well-educated Roman ladies, and much to Jerome's obvious approval, she had chosen to forgo her numerous advantages for a life of ascetic piety, during which Jerome became her instructor in the Scriptures. When Jerome fell out with Church officials in Rome, he chose to return to Bethlehem and, most significantly, Paula followed him there with one of her daughters. The rest of her children, we are told, were left weeping on the quayside for their departing mother.

Having forsaken her luxurious lifestyle and the rest of her family, Paula showed great commitment in learning Hebrew and assisting Jerome in his translation of the Bible from Greek and Hebrew into his Latin, Vulgate version. Paula worked alongside Jerome in Bethlehem for two decades, assisting him also in founding their own religious community in Bethlehem, setting up pilgrim hostels and monasteries there, and continued to do so until her death in AD 404. Evidence suggests that Paula found great peace and contentment in her new life and in a letter to Marcella, a family friend in Rome, she and her daughter Eustochium tried to persuade her to leave Rome and join them in the Holy Land. Paula's letter also poignantly high-

lights the contrast between the wealth of the Rome she had left
behind and her new, frugal, ascetic existence:

> Where are spacious porticoes? Where are gilded ceilings? Where
> are houses decorated by the sufferings and labours of condemned
> wretches? . . . In the village of Christ . . . all is rusticity, and except
> for psalms, silence . . . the ploughman, holding the plough handle,
> sings Alleluia; the perspiring reaper diverts himself with psalms.
> . . . Indeed, we do not think of what we are doing or how we
> look, but see only that for which we are longing.[10]

In a similar vein to Egeria's recording of the holy places for her
convent sisters, Paula and her daughter wrote an equally detailed
and evocative account that invited Marcella to participate in their
sacred pilgrimages on an emotional if vicarious level. Their
descriptions are infused with classical references, indicative of
Paula's considerable education; and she argues that all pilgrims now
choose to visit not Rome, but the sacred places of the Holy Land.

A widow of wealth and independence with the opportunity to
travel at least in a greater degree of comfort than most, Paula
forfeited family and home environment in Rome to embrace an
austere and relatively secluded life, devoid of the riches and servants
to which she had been accustomed. Further, many scholars maintain
that for several women such as Paula, it was the embracing of a life
of chastity with its denial of their sexuality that 'placed them outside
of the normal gender requirements of their culture and allowed them
the freedom to travel', otherwise Paula may have excited a somewhat different response when she chose to live among the Egyptian
monks![11] However, as Jerome tells us, she had by now become
'forgetful of her sex', she had become a vessal of the spirit and a
devotee of religious learning, electing not to return to Rome, but to
live out her life in Bethlehem, immersing herself wholeheartedly in
the customs, language and Christian iconography of her new
surroundings.

The relationship between Jerome and Paula is an intriguing one, if not simply one of mutual admiration between teacher and pupil. Depictions of Jerome rarely show him with Paula and her daughter, although one such portrayal, by Francesco Botticini, *St Jerome in Penitence with Saints and Donors*, can be viewed in the National Gallery, London, shows St Jerome in his scarlet robes with Paula and her daughter at his side.

Jerome's praise of Paula held her up as an example to contemporary women aspiring to undertake their own pilgrimage, particularly those devout widows with the means and the circumstances to make such an extended journey. His enthusiastic commendation was later to be parodied by Chaucer in his depiction of the infamous Wife of Bath. Not only does the Wife wear Jerome's characteristic scarlet, but Chaucer has her make frequent reference to Jerome in her Prologue, particularly to his treatise against marriage with its advocacy of perpetual chastity. In the mouth of the Wife of Bath Jerome's words are twisted and delivered as her own explosive and provocative views on sex and marriage. Her pilgrimage repertoire includes those same places Paula had visited fired with religious conviction, though clearly Chaucer's Wife embarked on her enterprise hoping for more worldly diversion.

Four centuries later, some further correspondence survives, this time relating to Anglo-Saxon women and pilgrimage. These exist as a corpus of letters concerning Pope Boniface VIII. At this time, the sacred centre of western Christianity was Rome, where the apostolic Ss Peter and Paul had been martyred. Revered for their sake, many lay folk and those from religious orders strove to make the pilgrimage there, some of these also choosing to make Rome their permanent residence, never to return.

Among the correspondence associated with St Boniface are intriguing letters, some by women planning to undergo pilgrimages, others by those who had returned, and another still requesting the advice of Boniface as to whether to undertake a pilgrimage at all.

The principal correspondents are all nuns: Eangyth, Ecgburg, Eadburga (probably most prolific since six of her letters survive), Aelffaed and Boniface himself. Eadburga had written to Boniface to seek guidance on a proposed pilgrimage to Rome and it is his reply of about AD 738 that we have. Boniface appears reluctant to commit himself either to encouraging or dissuading Eadburga. It seems that she was living in retirement at her monastery and that Boniface is undecided as to whether she would gain any greater peace or powers of contemplation were she to undertake a pilgrimage; however, he acknowledges that he had indeed witnessed the inner peace that others, such as one Sister Wiethburg, had derived from her visit to the holy places. A later letter indicates that Eadburga did in fact take her journey and met Boniface in Rome.

In another of the letters, an abbess named Eangyth seeks the guidance of Boniface when she finds herself overwhelmed with the responsibility of having to cope with her monastery's ailing fortunes and certain troublesome monks. She resolved to relinquish her responsibilities to her religious community and depart on pilgrimage to Rome with her daughter, but is eager for Boniface to furnish her with some divinely channelled guidance on the matter. It seems possible that given the exodus of many clerics, monks, nuns and lay folk to Rome at this time, many of whom chose to take up perm- anent residence there, that Eangyth saw her pilgrimage there as an opportunity for a fresh start and perhaps a better life for herself and her daughter. Unfortunately, no letters survive to indicate what path she chose, or what counsel Boniface offered.

Over the following centuries and as the freedom of movement of both nuns and women on pilgrimage became a more contested issue and subject to increasing restrictions, women mystics, anchoresses and wives and widows who chose to forsake their homes, opting instead for a chaste and ascetic existence, became more common. In later years such women might themselves become figures of veneration, just as the virgin martyrs, St Bridget and St Catherine, who had died for their faith and been canonised as saints, women who attracted considerable followings that in turn inspired new generations of women pilgrims. One such figurehead was Birgitta Birgersdotter (or Bridget), born in 1303 to a wealthy family connected to the Swedish royal house and with influence at court. At thirteen she was married, subsequently giving birth to eight children as well as serving at court. After a pilgrimage to the shrine of St Olaf in Trondheim, Norway, she undertook another, this time to Santiago de Compostela in north-western Spain with her husband when she was about forty. On their return, her husband fell ill and in 1344 Bridget was widowed. Outwardly she continued as before, but feeling the calling of a divine vocation and the futility of her existence without the renunciation and devotional practice with which she felt such an affinity, she began to busy herself with the founding of a new religious order.

Between 1344 and 1349 Bridget lived at the Cistercian monastery of Alvastra, Sweden's largest monastery, governed by St Bernard, during which time her devotional journey began in earnest. She reported a vision in which Christ spoke to her, electing her as his bride on account of her having forsaken all else on her husband's death and because of her intention to live a life of abstinence and divine love. Further to this mystical, spiritual union between Christ and Bridget, in a vision reminiscent of the divine instruction that led to the building of a holy house at Walsingham, Bridget said she was ordered by Christ to found a convent and appoint to it a mother and an abbess. The house was to be mainly for women, although men were also welcome, and would operate as a religious centre, encouraging the simple life and spiritual development.

Bridget's divine visions continued and were written down with the help of important Swedish ecclesiastics, among them Master Mathias, an Augustinian canon associated with the Dominicans, who translated the Bible into Swedish for her. Her visions were reportedly channelled through the Virgin Mary and Christ. They directed her religious life, but also became gradually more political in nature as Bridget's hunger for Church reform grew. Bridget recorded some of her visions in Swedish, while others were recorded by clerics until she herself became sufficiently adept at reading and writing Latin.

In 1349/1350, Bridget went to Rome in the year of the Jubilee or Holy Year to campaign for the Pope's imprimatur for her new religious order. However, the Pope now had his seat at Avignon and did not attend. Bridget was strongly concerned for the reinstatement of the Pope at Rome which would re-establish the city as the centre of Christianity. Consequently, she became something of a force to be reckoned with in ecclesiastical politics. Her visions also prompted her to rebuke the Swedish royal house for its dissipated lifestyle, although her strictures seem to have gone unheeded. She was also responsible for urging Pope Clement VI's interventin in securing a peace between England and France during the Hundred Years' War.

It was at Rome that Bridget decided to remain for the last years of her life, her visions now mostly reported to concern the necessity for reform within the Church, to be facilitated through the changing of the wordly ways of the Pope, cardinals and clergy. One such vision, purportedly channelled through the Virgin Mary, had to do with the importance of clerical celibacy:

You must also know that if any pope were to give priests licence to enter into carnal wedlock, he himself would be damned by God with a sentence, as would be applied to someone who had committed a great sin, and who by right should have his eyes plucked out, his lips cut off, with his nose and ears, his feet and hands, and whose corpse should be covered with blood and frozen with cold; and further, his dead body would be handed over to wild animals. And the same would happen to a pope who would give priests licence to marry, contrary to the above divine order, as this pope would be suddenly deprived of spiritual sight, of spiritual hearing, of spiritual words and spiritual works. And all of his spiritual wisdom would spiritually fail. And moreover, his soul would descend to hell, to be eternally tormented there as a prey for the demons.[12]

Bridget's religious order was approved in 1370, but she did not see the Pope's return to Rome. Between 1372 and 1373 she set out on a pilgrimage from her new residence in Rome to the Holy Land. Here she followed the Via Dolorosa, the path that Christ had taken to Calvary, in a spiritual re-creation of Christ's suffering which she experienced on an emotional level reminiscent of Paula, so that she 'saw' the scourging in Pilate's courtyard, Christ carrying the Cross, and witnessed his agonising and protracted death.

This imaginative, emotional revisiting of the Holy Land's sacred places is also familiar through a study of Margery Kempe's accounts of her experience, in which the affective piety of Bridget is apparently replicated in Kempe's own, somewhat overly theatrical displays at the sites of Christ's suffering. Bridget's response had been magnified by the Virgin affording her an explicitly detailed vision of the sufferings of her Son:

> First they fixed His right hand to the tree, in which holes had been drilled for the nails, and they pierced His hand at the point where the bone was firmest. Next they stretched His other hand with a rope . . . Then they crucified His right foot with two nails . . . After doing this they put the crown of thorns on His head, and it pricked my Son's venerable head so fiercely that His eyes were filled with the flowing blood, His ears were blocked and His beard utterly defaced by the blood running down.[13]

Bridget's *Liber Celestis Revelaciones* or 'Revelations' as they are often referred to today, consisted of some 700 such transcribed visions which were edited, collated and then circulating posthumously in Latin. By 1380, further materials were published pertaining to her letters and visions concerning political and clerical leaders and the reforms she had attempted to enforce on them.

Bridget lived humbly in relative poverty, caring for the poor and for pilgrims. Her deeds, as her life, were profoundly influenced by the counsel and supervision proffered by her visions. She was also to offer one such vision of the Virgin as counsel to wives, widows and virgins:

> For there is no mother who loves my Son above all things and asks the same of her children, but that I am immediately ready to help her to effect what she asks. There is also no widow who firmly prays for the help of God to remain in her widowhood consecrated to God until her death, but that I am immediately ready to fulfil her will with her. . . . There is also no virgin who desires to keep her maidenhead to God to her death, but that I am ready to defend her and to comfort her . . .[14]

Under the guidance of Bishop Alfonso, Bridget was still going on pilgrimages at about the age of seventy when she went to Bethlehem and Jerusalem to fulfil a vow. It was not until several years after her death, on 23 July 1373 in Rome, that a request for her canonisation was made to Pope Boniface IX, and on 7 October 1391 she was made a saint. As a result, the convent Bridget had founded in Vadstena in southern Sweden now had a saint as patron and the convent and its church were to place Vadstena firmly on the pilgrimage trail. In the same way that Walsingham became established as 'England's Nazareth', the small town of Vadstena came to be known as the 'Rome of the North'. In Rome itself, the Swedish hospital of St Bridget was located in the area where she had lived towards the latter part of her life and was run by her namesake, the Bridgettine Order. Their rules concerning hospitality to be offered to the pilgrim stated that they should be given free wine and bread for the first three days of their stay, and that they should be allowed to reside there as long as they chose. As with most pilgrim hostelries founded by religious orders, only the rich were asked to make a donation to cover their stay. Today, St Bridget continues to be associated with pilgrimage and is depicted wearing Bridgettine robes, with a cross and holding a book or pilgrim's staff.

THREE

'Wykked Wyves' – Portrayals and Perceptions of Women Pilgrims

Some women travel on pilgrimages away from town in order to frolic and kick up their heels in jolly company. But this is only sin and folly. It is a sin to use God as excuse and shelter for frivolity.[1]

While playing an integral part in the practise of medieval pilgrimage, women generally receive less mention, and the surviving documents and accounts of real-life women pilgrims are somewhat eclipsed by those of their male counterparts. We sometimes have to look to records by others, as well as our own powers of discernment, to appreciate that women went on pilgrimage with men, stood shoulder to shoulder with them in the crowds gathered to witness holy relics, journeyed side-by-side with them on the roads to their destinations and were fellow-travellers aboard the galleys that carried pilgrims to the Holy Land. This sort of detective work is vital in a study of medieval pilgrimage where specific reference to women pilgrims can be scant and generalised; it is important to keep in mind that all such experiences described by male travellers who recorded their journeys, or that are provided in other documentation, were also those of women. Significantly, as a practice predominantly engaged in by men, for women to go on pilgrimage meant that they crossed several of the rigid boundaries that normally operated to compart-mentalise the behaviour of the sexes in everyday society; it opened up the experience to everyone: 'this day more than 200 pilgrims from Paris arrived . . . men, women and people of good standing . . . and among them were men and women well dressed and well mounted and very honourable . . .',[2] words that highlight the mix of men and women, humble and high born, that went to a single shrine in Italy.

Those, comparatively fewer, extant personal accounts, letters and documents that pertain to women pilgrims do, nevertheless, furnish us with a colourful insight into their many guises and experiences, whether as fervent and pious subjects – 'women in compunction of heart' – as zealous and determined travellers, or as nurturing mothers and wives praying for their families at chosen shrines. However, it is narrative and social commentary that tend to offer us the most elaborate representations of the woman on pilgrimage.

The ironically titled *Quinze Joies de Mariage*, or 'Fifteen Joys of Marriage', offered a humorous, if sardonic view of the role of the husband who accompanied his wife on pilgrimage when it came to the purchase of souvenirs at the various shrines. However, it perhaps unwittingly serves too to emphasise the spiritual ardour and resolve of the woman pilgrim.

And here they arrived at Le Puy in the Auvergne . . . God knows how crushed and pushed about the poor husband is in the middle of the crowd in order to get his wife through! . . . God knows that he is well jostled and gets some good elbowing and is nicely buffeted! Furthermore, there are among the women there with them some rich ladies, maidens and bourgeoises who are buying beads of coral, jade or amber and rings and other jewels. So his wife must have them like the others; sometimes, there's no more money, but nevertheless, he's got to get them.[3]

The accounts of the Dominican friar Felix Fabri, who made two pilgrimages to the Holy Land in the fifteenth century, vividly record his experiences in line with a promise he had made to his brethren at Ulm. One episode in particular highlights the immense enthusiasm and vigour with which women might embark on pilgrimage, sometimes to the annoyance of their companions. On a boat on his second trip to the Holy Land in 1483, he complains of the wife of a Flemish pilgrim who is 'restless and inquisitive', running up and down the ship in her efforts not to miss anything:

> She ran hither and thither incessantly about the ship, and was full of curiosity . . . and made herself hated exceedingly. Her husband seemed to be a decent man, and for his sake many held their tongues; but had he not been there it would have gone hard with her. This woman was a thorn in the eyes of us all.[4]

It seems that apart from the woman's agitated inquisitiveness that so irritated her male companions, she had already caused discomfort by being the only woman aboard: 'When this woman came on board many were vexed at it, because she was the only one on board, for before her there was no woman among us . . . and at the thought of one woman having to dwell alone among so many noblemen . . .'[5]

There is a suggestion in Fabri's observations that despite the classless nature of pilgrimage practice, some class and gender friction might well surface within an enclosed setting such as on board a pilgrim galley. Brother Fabri infers that it was not fitting for her to be aboard as the only woman among the men, particularly among noblemen. However, as he explains, the captain of the accompanying galley had taken all the other women of the party on to his own vessel so we may infer that as she was in the company of her husband, she had been ordered to board where there was space, on Fabri's boat. It is also interesting to note here that efforts had been made by the other ship's captain to keep the women pilgrims together by taking them as a group aboard his own ship.

It appears from Fabri's account that it is only the presence of her Flemish husband '[who] seemed to be a decent man', that prevents the other men from acting against her. One may assume that without this there could have been all manner of objection by the noblemen, similar to the protests of the nobles in another of Fabri's accounts who refuse to board a galley occupied by an elderly woman.

Nor was it unheard of for women to be isolated by their male fellow pilgrims. This happened to Margery Kempe who was abandoned several times by the party with whom she was travelling, but also on account of their aggravation at her relentless enthusiasm:

> And soon after, some of the company she trusted best, and also her own maidservant, said she should not accompany them any longer. . . . And then one of them, who was looking after her money, very angrily left her a noble to go where she liked and shift for herself as well as she could – for with them, they said, she could stay no longer, and they abandoned her that night.[6]

However, another early pilgrim, the fourth-century Spanish nun Egeria, discussed in the previous chapter, is lavishly praised by the monk Valerius, who tells his brethren how she 'transformed the weakness of her sex into an iron strength, that she might win the reward of eternal life'.[7]

One might imagine that given the hardships and challenges that pilgrimage presented, both mentally and physically, women and men alike would often be hard pressed to survive in the unfamiliar even dangerous terrain of the Holy Land, or simply to fulfil the object of their destination. While pilgrim companionship might lift the spirits and provide an air of camaraderie among pilgrim bands, those of varying degrees of physical capability would travel together. As the minority and the perceived 'weaker sex', women perhaps had more to prove in relation to their physical capability to meet the rigours of pilgrimage and so it is likely that particular examples of their courage and perseverance would be duly noted, even held up for emulation.

Fabri's description of the somewhat strenuous donkey ride to Jerusalem from the port of Jaffa indicates the discomforts that might be encountered:

> The roads in this desert are stony, generally high and narrow, with deep valleys on either hand, so that, should the beast fall down the steep stones he would fall into some deep abyss, and man and beast perish together. I wondered at the women who accompanied us, that they should ride so boldly, seeing that a woman is timid by nature.[8]

Fabri also describes the ardour of a group of older women whom he encountered on his journey:

> certain women well-stricken in years, wealthy matrons, six in number, were there together with us, desiring to cross the sea to the holy places. I was astonished at the courage of these old women, who through old age were scarcely able to support their own weight, yet forgot their own frailty, and through love for the Holy Land joined themselves to young knights and underwent the labours of strong men.[9]

As it happens, the ship is about to be boarded by a group of young noblemen on their way to receive their knighthoods. They object to the women being on board, deeming it inappropriate that they should share their passage with a group of old women when they are en route to receive such an honour. The women stalwartly remain on board and are levelly defended by some other knights who praise their piety, arguing that everyone's sea journey might be made the safer for it. Eventually, the nobles retreat in defeat and Fabri tells us that 'those devout ladies' remained his companions on board ship both on the outward and return journeys.

Such courage and determination were also exhibited by women pilgrims confronted with risk or danger. For pilgrims coming ashore from an overseas voyage, this might include the moment at which they are called on to jump from the galley into a waiting boat that would take them to shore. When the water was choppy, this had to be a correctly calculated leap to avoid landing badly on one's face or back and literally missing the boat, a leap that one account tells us some male pilgrims declined, judging it safer to stay on board and forgo the chance to stretch their legs ashore. Again, it is the courage of the women pilgrims on board that is brought to our attention: 'I have seen women who at first were full of fears, and scarcely dared to look at the sea, who nevertheless became so bold by practice that they would venture to jump from a galley into a boat.'[10]

By its very nature, pilgrimage required its participants, whether men or women, to overcome the same fears or physical challenges. It could also constitute an act of penance, whether self-imposed or otherwise. While the majority of pilgrims undertook their journeys on foot, those whose path was actually trodden barefoot were particularly revered. There were women too who chose this harsh course, among them the Countess of Clare, born in 1295 to Princess Joan, daughter of Edward I, and Gilbert de Clare. On their way to the Walsingham shrine, many pilgrims would pass the so-called Slipper Chapel where they would take off and leave their shoes before walking the rest of the way, 'the Holy Mile' to Walsingham, barefoot.

However, in contrast to the praise of women pilgrims by the monk Valerius, St Jerome and by Fabri, there are also several fictional depictions designed to show women pilgrims in a far less favourable light.

The previously mentioned fifteenth-century French satire on wives entitled 'The Fifteen Joys of Marriage' includes several such portrayals. At the time it was written, the efficacy of pilgrimage was being reassessed by the Church and criticised by various commentators who highlighted abuses of its privileges. Pilgrim shrines, their relics, profiteering clerics and pilgrims themselves were all held to account. Set against this backdrop, the *Fifteen Joys* uses female characters to expound some of these themes. For example, it illustrates those women who embark on their pilgrimage without any spiritual motive, using it instead as a means of sexual and profane entertainment. For each of the joys, the suffering and discomfort of the husband in his association with such a woman is emphasised, finishing with the formula, 'ains y finera en languissant miserablement ses jours' – in such a way he ends his days, languishing in misery and torment.[11]

The eighth joy tells of a woman who makes a vow in childbirth which she later uses to force her husband to allow her to make pilgrimage to the shrine of Le Puy. She pretends that their child is ill in order to convince him that she must go, thus evading her domestic responsibilities; she torments him until he concedes. The message here is that wives choose to go on pilgrimages only 'because they cannot do as they will in their own homes'. The husband accompanies his wife to Le Puy experiencing much tribulation at her hand on the way. He struggles through the heaving crowds to ensure that her girdle and rosary are brought into contact with the holy relics and then, buffeted and jostled again, is forced to re-enter the fray to purchase her desired coral rosaries and trinkets, the favourite souvenirs of the rich women among the pilgrims. We are told that 'le bon homme est foullé et debouté dans la presse', trampled and shoved by the expectant crowd, and re-emerges the poorer in pocket for it. The tale continues with the couple producing further offspring, so fulfilling the tale's rationale – the husband has become ensnared in the wife's 'trap'. The 'Joy' is rendered with ironic humour, but was surely also intended as a familiar, if not cautionary sequence of events for its male audience.

In another of the 'Joys' (the twelfth), we encounter the popular anti-female scenario of the hen-pecked husband in a household where the perceived 'proper' order of things has been turned upside down and the wife holds the reins. In this tale, the wife employs devious means to rid herself of her husband, sending him off on a pilgrimage she had vowed to go on herself, but that she finds herself incapable of undertaking due to a supposed pain in her side! The husband obliges by setting out on the arduous pilgrimage in his wife's place and the tale concludes by once again stating that marriage can only be a source of eternal misery and sadness for the husband.

The wife who figures in the eleventh joy uses pilgrimage for an altogether different purpose, though again to further her own ends. She resourcefully employs the journey as a means to secure herself a mate. Having become pregnant by one man who refuses to marry her, the protagonist takes the counsel of an older woman who advises her on how to ensnare herself a husband. Through calculated and flirtatious means, their victim finds himself quickly smitten, while the woman snuggles up close behind him on their horse so that he becomes 'tout alumé et embrasé de l'amour d'elle'. Once he is ensnared the pair are made man and wife. Only a few months after they are wed, the wife gives birth to the child, product of her previous dalliance, by which time all is lost for her new, unsuspecting spouse, who realises that he has been duped.

In a reversal of the narrative device of the 'Fifteen Joys of Marriage', another contemporary text, 'Le Ménagier de Paris', was written as a cautionary tale to a younger wife by her husband, again using pilgrimage as its vehicle. He related to her the account of a young wife who attempted to run away from her husband in search of a younger lover. Unfortunately, the wife finds herself abandoned by her paramour and forced into prostitution on the streets of Avignon. On discovering the predicament of his young wife, the husband sends her brothers to her amid the spreading rumours and gossip about her reversal of fortune. They use the cover of pilgrimage as their disguise, dressing the young wife in pilgrim's garb with coarse cloak and St James's cockleshell, while the husband loudly voices his relief that his wife has been returned to him safely from her pilgrimage. Her reputation is restored by virtue of the symbolic nature of the pilgrim's dress and the husband has thus delivered his moralising and cautionary message to his young wife.

Thus, while there were pilgrims such as Fabri and Jerome who took the time to expound the virtues of some of the women pilgrims they encountered, popular literature was to play a potent role in subverting any such positive portrayals and naturally, having a wider audience, had a significant impact on medieval opinion. By its very nature, such literature often undermined any genuine devotion or vivacity that women may have displayed on such journeys, using the women instead as the subjects for morality tales, cautionary teachings and the continuation of those misogynistic themes established in earlier writings. Within the context of the widespread belief in women's weakness and the long-sustained argument for the sins of Eve, it would have been deemed inappropriate for women to receive lavish praise for their endeavours, unless perhaps they were wholly to relinquish their sexuality and physical connection with society by embracing chastity, seclusion or consigning their lives to a religious order, as in the cases of Paula and Egeria.

In this way sacred literature inadvertently competed with the popular perception of the female pilgrim as wayward or untrustworthy, in that it held up for emulation the lives of those women who had been canonised for their profound asceticism – their self-deprivation, physical detachment from the world, denial of their sexuality and acts of unwavering faith. In fact, using the Wife of Bath as his mouthpiece, Chaucer states that women were rarely accorded such merit or praise unless they were saints:

> For trusteth wel, it is an impossible
> That any clerk wol speke good of wives,
> But if it be of hooly seintes lives . . .[12]

In a book of moralising teachings, Geoffrey de La Tour-Landry compiled several edifying lessons for his motherless daughters, designed to shape their better conduct, preserve their good reputation, as well as make them desirable wives. He cites the lives of the female saints on many occasions, encouraging his daughters to conduct their own lives 'as haue done these holy wymmen, lyke as it is conteyned in the legendis, and in the lyues of the sayntes of heuen'.[13]

As a saint for whom many women felt an affinity, St Katherine of Alexandria was held up as a particular example by La Tour-Landry in his fourteenth-century instruction on the reasons for sending children to school:

> as dyde saynt katheryn, whiche thurgh her wysedome and by her clergye, with the grace of the holy ghoost, surmounted and vaynquysshed the wysest men of al grece. . . . And the begynnyng and fundament of the knowlege of god she had thurgh the clergye where as she knewe the trouthe & the sauement of her self.[14]

Saints' legends and lives were the source for a host of such women saints who had also been pilgrims, lending considerable credibility to their journeys as a spiritual exercise that could be safely held up for emulation. These were women driven by religious fervour who went about their pilgrimages with unwavering faith in the spiritual efficacy of their journeys. A group of such women, thought to be in their eighties, is described among one pilgrim party immersing themselves in the waters of the River Jordan: 'nothing is wont to befall those who gravely and devoutly baptize themselves, as we see in the case of women pilgrims, who bathed among the reeds above us with modesty, silence, and devotion, and far more sedately than we . . .'[15]

Such pious fervour was also thought to be behind some female pilgrims' determination to overcome the obstacles they faced and push themselves to the limits of their endurance. Egeria describes her own ascent of Mount Sinai as a journey that required great exertion, 'but though I had to go on foot I was not conscious of the effort – in fact I hardly noticed it because, by God's will, I was seeing my hopes come true'.[16]

In a society in which women were rarely praised for their virtue, the stories of female saints could serve as the inspiration for some. One such woman was Margery Kempe. She tried desperately to emulate the lives of holy figures, seeking out the counsel of women visionaries and anchoresses in order to shape her own moral conduct and in an endeavour to win the admiration of the priests and clergy whom she met along the way. In an almost unceasing effort to gain endorsement for herself as the pious and devoutly spiritual woman she believed herself to be, Margery's accounts continually seek to justify her words, deeds and thoughts, however outlandish, as if guided by God, the Holy Spirit and the saints.

Many men and women had chosen pilgrimage for its opportunities to make new acquaintances and to live outside the constraints of their usual existence for a while. Epitomising this approach were those very pilgrims encountered by Margery Kempe in Venice who had elected on their pilgrimage to eat, drink and be merry in their new company, not wishing to be reminded of the scriptural significance of their destinations, or indeed to recognise the prescribed, religious reasons for their being there.

FOUR

The Theatre of Devotion – Margery Kempe

And when this creature saw Jerusalem – she was riding on an ass – she thanked God with all her heart. . . . Then for the joy that she had and the sweetness that she felt in the conversation of our Lord, she was on the point of falling off her ass. . . .[1]

Margery Kempe's dictated fifteenth-century account of her journey to Rome, Assisi, the Holy Land and beyond, offers a valuable resource for a study of what it meant to be a woman on medieval pilgrimage. Indeed, for the two previous centuries no written account survives of an Englishwoman's pilgrimage to Jerusalem; in fact, the manuscript itself subsequently lay undiscovered for 500 years, until 1934. Today, Kempe's work is considered the earliest autobiographical work in English that we have.

After the failure of her brewery business in King's Lynn, Norfolk, Margery left her husband and family (settling the family debts before she left) and set out alone on her first pilgrimage. Her

43

accounts, dictated in all their unembarrassed detail, are an edifying source on the dangers and pitfalls peculiar to women on pilgrimage, as well as providing evidence of the resourcefulness women pilgrims showed in overcoming them and completing their journeys. Before she embarked on her pilgrimages, Margery Kempe had already experienced a full and eventful life, running several businesses and raising fourteen children, as well as having been subject to bouts of misdiagnosed illness during which she was kept under lock and key.

Margery was born in the town of Bishop's-Lynn (now King's Lynn), in about 1373, the daughter of John Brunham, a well-respected city mayor and Member of Parliament. Although hers was an important family in the town, Margery was apparently not taught to read or write, hence the dictation of her accounts to two scribes when she was in her sixties. Aged about twenty, she married John Kempe. It was with the birth of her first child that some of her mental and emotional difficulties began to surface, difficulties that would manifest themselves thereafter throughout her travels as a pilgrim.

Given that childbirth was a dangerous and traumatic experience for both mother and baby in medieval England, with poor hygiene and limited knowledge of safe procedure, it is perhaps not surprising that Margery suffered a particularly distressing time. She became morbidly obsessed with the fear of her own death through the delivery of her baby, so much so that she called in a confessor. She survived the birth only to suffer what we might consider today a mental breakdown and post-partum psychosis, perhaps more commonly known as post-natal depression. Since this was not a recognised condition at the time, Margery's depression, delirium and self-destructive, even suicidal, tendencies were interpreted by her husband and those around her rather differently. Instead of giving the care and support that was called for, fearing for her safety, her husband ordered that she be kept under lock and key and physically restrained to prevent her from harming herself. Her condition was exacerbated by the fact that, like one possessed, she reported simultaneous visions of the Devil and Hell.

It was while suffering thus that Margery received her first 'visitation' from Christ, 'in the likeness of a man, the most seemly, most beauteous . . . clad in a mantle of purple silk, sitting upon her bedside'.[2] This was an epiphany for Margery and occasioned a profound spiritual conversion, one that shaped the ascetically pious Margery Kempe whom we have come to know through her pilgrimage accounts.

After her recovery and visitation, Margery became a changed woman. She goes on a shopping spree for fine clothes, fashionably slashed to reveal the bright silks underneath, and she embarks on two new business ventures. The first was a brewery, a business which she entered into with her husband, with herself as the principal. For several years the brewery flourished, only to founder later at great financial loss and much to her disappointment.

It is through these early episodes of Margery's life that we may begin to gauge her state of mind, her sensibilities and insecurities. She craves the respect and admiration of those around her and, at this stage in her life, is clearly a woman of great pride. Her over-dressing in sumptuous new attire and conspicuous *crespinettes* (lavish headpieces with gold pipes and wires) incited the gossip and envy of her neighbours, which Margery felt very keenly. However, she transmutes their hostility to a spiritual end, interpreting it as 'the scourges of our Lord' meted out to her on account of her pride and covetousness. She was obviously, too, a particularly enterprising woman, following her brewery business with a new project, the opening of a corn mill and the purchase of two horses. However, when that venture also failed, she tells us that she chose to forsake worldly things to enter the 'way of the everlasting life as shall be told hereafter'.

Unfortunately, Margery's accounts are not chronologically arranged, being instead a hotchpotch of different sequences from her life that jump between past and present. However, it is possible to make out the patterns of her life and her pilgrimage journeys, as well as the process that culminated in her setting out on pilgrimage without her husband. Margery subjected herself to an intense cycle of fasting, confession and the wearing of a hair shirt, during which she experienced frequent temptations and mystical visions. Her dictated experiences are very reminiscent of those of so many other, earlier, women martyrs and saints with which Margery would have been familiar. Such women as Catherine of Siena (1347–80), for example, who had fasted with such vigour that it is thought she may have starved herself to death. Catherine also dictated an account of her life, meditations and revelations, in her case to her confessor and biographer Raimondo.

Margery's behaviour in church became increasingly characterised by seemingly uncontrollable emotional outbursts and 'weepings', which elicited considerable disapproval wherever she went. Christ appeared to her to counsel that she should do away with her hair shirt and stop her ceaseless saying of the rosary; instead, she should take a confessor, an (unnamed) anchorite in Lynn, and abstain from meat. Nonetheless, her outbursts became more agitated and violent; to the modern ear they sound alarmingly similar to the onset of a fit, even of an epileptic seizure. She is described as flailing her arms about, with her body wresting from one side to the other. She takes on a waxy appearance 'blue and livid, like the colour of lead', while she weeps and yells. There is some evidence to suggest the possibility that epilepsy is a symptom of a desire to purge oneself of guilt or perceived defilement, so that the subject is wrested free of their burden. Certainly, Margery was ever conscious of the weight of sin and also mentions on more than one occasion a childhood incident of which she is deeply ashamed and which is always on her mind, but is not divulged. The response of those around her, however, was to interpret her abnormal behaviour as madness or possession and she was spat on, banned from certain places, cursed and scorned. Only those few men of God and those who truly believed her to be the holy woman she professed herself to be interpreted Margery's struggle as a sign of God's presence. For the modern audience it is impossible to tell whether she really was exhibiting signs of spiritual turmoil or whether Margery Kempe had simply become adept at stage-managing a show of emotion and possession by God's spirit or, indeed, whether she was an unfortunate sufferer of fits, epilepsy, even schizophrenia. If the latter was the case, then it only served to exacerbate Margery's situation; as with her apparent post-natal depression, since schizophrenia was not recognised, its symptoms were labelled as madness or, worse, interpreted as far more sinister evidence of consorting with the Devil.

In Book XXXV, Margery relates other 'symptoms' of her divine possession that might be interpreted, as some scholars have done, as indicating a medical condition. In a similar way, those symptoms noted by Hildegard of Bingen (1098–1179), the twelfth-century visionary mystic, have led some to dub her the 'most distinguished migraine sufferer'. Those symptoms reported by Margery included that 'Sometimes she heard with her bodily ears such sounds and melodies that she could not hear what anyone said to her at that time unless he spoke louder', 'sweet smells in her nose' and a burning sensation in her chest. Others still may appear to the modern reader as natural occurrences that have been transformed in Margery's mind into something more ethereal, in line with her passionate belief, 'She saw with her bodily eyes many white things flying all about her . . . as specks in a sunbeam . . . and the brighter the sun shone, the better she could see them.'[3]

For Margery, however, her experiences were very real and she reports such astonishing episodes as that of being invited to a virtual re-enactment of the births of the Virgin, at which she is assistant midwife, of John the Baptist and finally of Christ. Later in the same Book, Christ accepts Margery as his mystical bride in spiritual marriage, an experience reminiscent of those of earlier mystics, in this case Margery's heroine, St Bridget of Sweden.

Certainly such episodes could lead Margery into trouble: in Canterbury she is accused of being a heretic as a result and in Leicester she is arrested, detained and questioned before being allowed to continue her journey. Margery's volatile, emotional

behaviour frequently led to serious misgivings about her orthodoxy. That she had become independent of her husband in an unconventional way may well have been deemed a threat to the existing social structure, in much the same way as breakaway movements such as the Lollards were perceived, one of whom she is indeed accused of being. This notion of Margery as a threat to order is supported by the account of her arrival in the next town, where the inhabitants beg her to give up her unusual wanderings and return home to her husband, to spin and weave as other women do. When she provoked the hostility of the monks at Canterbury Cathedral, it may have been because they considered her a disruptive influence on the efficient passage of pilgrims to the shrine of St Thomas, the monks' primary concern.

Another significant turning point on Margery's elected spiritual path was her fixation with the idea of regaining her chastity, and she pleaded with her husband to abstain from physical contact with her. St Bridget, one of Margery's holy female influences, had also taken up the chaste life, in her case after the death of her husband. Even within marriage she had considered sex as 'inordinate love', unless for the purpose of procreation. In the early summer of 1413, Margery's husband finally consented to a vow of chastity within their marriage on condition that she give up her Friday fasting so that they might once more dine together, and also if she would settle his debts. (Margery came into an inheritance on the death of her father at the end of this year.)

It is shortly after this that Margery claimed that she had been called by God to visit the religious sites of Rome, Santiago de Compostela and Jerusalem on pilgrimage. It is also at this stage in her narration that Margery describes an intriguing episode. She recounts how she is warmly welcomed to dine with some monks and speaks to them, she says, as guided by God. One of the monks is therefore prompted to ask her advice on the state of his spiritual morality. Margery is able to tell the monk that she sees he has sinned in lechery and in the 'keeping of worldly goods'. Astonished, the monk tests Margery by asking her to tell him whether it was with married or single women that he had sinned, to which she replies 'Sir, with wives'. The monk is fully repentant and seeks forgiveness.

Kempe is encouraged to undertake her pilgrimage to the Holy Land, guided also by the spiritual counsel of such mystics as Dame Julian of Norwich, who tells her she should follow Christ's divine instruction, and by a Carmelite, William Southfield, who again endorses her proposed course of action. In late 1413, Margery arrived in Constance in Germany and from there travelled on to Venice via Bologna. At Venice we witness Margery embroiled in a characteristic scuffle with her pilgrim companions. Beginning in Constance, her maidservant and the party she is travelling with had become unsettled by her 'weeping and violent sobbing' and the fact that she refused to eat meat with them. They abandon her, refusing to allow her to travel in their company any longer and they take her maidservant from her so that 'she would not be prostituted in her company'.

While Margery's affective piety might be deemed a little excessive, the reaction of her companions is indicative of the wide chasm that could exist between pilgrims, illustrated by the varying depths of their religious commitment. When she meets up with the group in Bologna, they allow her back among them on one condition, 'you will not talk of the Gospel where we are, but you will sit and make merry, like us, at all meals'.[4] Clearly, with this party Margery is in the minority as a pilgrim devoting her entire energies to the spiritual purpose in hand, emotionally responsive to the spiritual prompts of the holy places she visits and fully confident of the efficacy of her pilgrimage.

On the advice of one of the more kindly members of the party, Margery begs to be allowed to travel on with them. She does so, but her companions continually jibe at her, treat her as their fool and make her sit at the lower end of the table. Margery's quiet endurance of such treatment gives some idea of what worse she might have encountered as a women left to travel on her own, for she is prepared to suffer such ordeals rather than risk being left to her own devices. When she is finally abandoned by this party at Venice, she is left to travel in the company of only one man, who, to her relief, had offered himself as her guide in light of what had happened. However, she is in very low spirits as they set off, on account, she says, of being in a strange country, not knowing the language or, indeed, her escort.

Margery's fears for her safety and the preservation of her new-found chastity are prevalent themes in her recounting of events and serve to reflect the inherent dangers of pilgrimage travel for women, particularly if they are not part of a larger, stronger company. She cites the 'indecent looks' directed at her by her male companions which made her fearful for her chastity. On one occasion, at a hostel on her way to Aachen and again deserted by the rest of her company, Kempe requests that the lady of the house allow her to have some of the maids to sleep in her bed with her for security. Although her request is met, she is still unable to sleep for fear of being violated. She repeated this practice compulsively: 'She dared trust no man; whether she had reason or not, she was always afraid. She scarcely dared sleep any night. . . .'[5]

Throughout the account, there are allusions as well as direct references to other dangers that might befall women (and pilgrims in general), of all of which Margery appears keenly aware. She perceives the danger, for example, of being robbed for a ring that she carries and tells us how she had 'much thought how she should keep this ring from being stolen on her travels'. Hence, when she is lodged in Venice at a good man's house, one morning she is thrown into disarray when she discovers it is not where she left it. Much to her relief, it is eventually found on the floorboards under her bed.

Illness was another consideration when travelling to lands, climates and to eat diets to which the pilgrim was not accustomed, the Holy Land presenting the most challenging combination of the three. Margery's accounts focus largely on her spiritual experiences of the holy places, only rarely offering us glimpses into the personal and physical aspects of the journey, but we know that many pilgrims suffered from heat exhaustion and food poisoning. Indeed, the account by William Wey, intended as a guide for pilgrims to the Holy Land, listed those foods to be avoided there on account of the likelihood of their causing the pilgrim serious illness:

> beware of fruytes that ye ete none for no thynge. As melons and suche colde fruytes, for they be not accordynge to our complexyon & they gendre a blody fluxe [diarrhoea]. And yf ony enghysshe man catche there that syknesse, it is a grete merueylle but yt he deye therof.[6]

Margery also recounts how even before reaching the Holy Land, when they stop at Venice, many of her companions have fallen ill after their sea voyage. The galleys that carried pilgrims across the sea to Venice and then on to the port of Jaffa often presented squalid, unsanitary conditions, partly due to the number of pilgrims aboard. Moreover, the pilgrims now had to contend with the sea and several accounts survive that tell of pilgrims dying in the midst of great storms, from sea-sickness, by drowning and even in shipwrecks. Equally, the conditions on board were not conducive to the sanitary preservation of food, with meat turning putrid or becoming worm-infested and water fetid. Clearly concerned at the condition of her fellow passengers at Venice, Margery is assured by Christ's voice, 'Don't be afraid, daughter, no one will die in the ship that you are in.'

Inevitably, pilgrims would also cross paths with other pilgrims of varying degrees of poverty or cleanliness. On one occasion, Margery falls into company with some poor pilgrims who were sustaining themselves on their journey by begging. They are also flea-ridden and are forced to regularly undress in front of her in order to pick themselves free of vermin. Unfortunately, some of these are passed to Margery so that she is bitten and stung day and night until she tells us, 'God sent her other companions'.

Given that many of Margery's pious outbursts were the result of spiritual prompts, her experience in the Holy Land, the place of Christ's birth, life and death, was naturally replete with regular bouts of weeping and breaking down, a train of events that started with her first glimpse of the Holy City:

And so they went on into the Holy Land until they could see Jerusalem. And when this creature saw Jerusalem – she was riding on an ass . . . for the joy that she had and the sweetness that she felt . . . she was on the point of falling off her ass. Then two German pilgrims went up to her and kept her from falling . . . thinking she was ill. . . .[7]

Several times, Margery mentally re-creates and emotionally relives the experience of the birth of Christ and his Passion through her visits to such sites as the Holy Sepulchre and Mount Calvary. 'The crying was so loud and so amazing that it astounded people . . . and she had them so often that they made her very weak in her bodily strength, especially if she heard of the Lord's Passion.'[8]

At the place of Christ's crucifixion she contemplates the moment when Christ is nailed to the Cross and is again overcome with grief, visualising his 'precious tender body, all rent and torn with scourges' as if He were there in front of her. Despite exhausting herself by her emotional outpourings, there can be no denying Margery's devotion and commitment to her pilgrimage, as well as her stamina and determination. The Holy Land could be almost unbearably hot and its terrain harsh and difficult to cover, especially for the inexperienced traveller such as most pilgrims were. Margery was in her sixties at this stage and shows great zeal in the physical energy she musters, for example in conquering Mount Sinai, notorious for its steep and demanding climb. In fact, when she beseeches her fellow pilgrims to assist her ascent, they are unable to oblige, having enough difficulty themselves. Eventually a chivalrous Saracen comes to her aid! – 'just then, a Saracen, a good *walking - hardship*

looking man, happened to come by her, and she put a groat into his hand . . . quickly the Saracen took her under his arm and led her up the high mountain . . .'.[9]

In fact, Margery Kempe regularly confesses to difficulty in keeping up with her male companions and enduring as long a day's walking as they are able. The revelation that she is normally unaccustomed to walking and is advancing in years must have mirrored the circumstance of many female pilgrims who undertook such journeys, perhaps as widows, and who might normally be used to considerable less physical exertion and without the need for such sustained stamina.

At Assisi, where Margery arrives in August 1414 in time to receive the St Lammas Day indulgence, she acquired the assistance and patronage of a Roman matron, Margaret Florentyne, with whom she travelled some of the way to Rome, enjoying the protection of Margaret's large retinue of Knights of Rhodes and her 'very fine equipage'. At Rome, she stayed in the English foundation of the Hospital of St Thomas of Canterbury. Here she resided comfortably enough, receiving communion each Sunday with her customary weeping, until a priest, apparently unnerved by her religious transports, successfully speaks out against her and she is thrown out. This becomes the common pattern of Margery's journeying – she is accepted, loved and assisted by some, shamed, insulted and abandoned by others in a never-ending cycle of comfort and rejection. Margery is fortunate enough to meet up with Margaret Florentyne again in Rome where she becomes her guest for dinner every Sunday. She is also invited back to the Hospital of St Thomas from whence she had been ejected, prompted by its recognition of Margery's charitable works in Rome.

Kempe becomes acquainted with a German-born priest, Wenslawe, attached to St John in the Lateran in Rome, and their relations present an interesting scenario, as well as a change of direction for Margery. To overcome their language barrier, they speak through an interpreter and Wenslawe seems to take great interest in Margery, particularly in her affective displays of piety. Rather than accept or reject Margery with the alacrity of others whom she has met, he tests Margery for any 'hypocritical pretence' by administering the sacrament to her away from the rest of the crowds, when everyone had gone home. Margery does not disappoint and bursts into copious weeping. The priest is utterly convinced that her reaction is the work of the Holy Ghost rather than mere theatrical display indulged in for the benefit of others. He requests her to put aside her white robes and encourages her to serve an impoverished woman in Rome as part of her penance. This she does for six weeks in what becomes an even greater test of her dedication. She sleeps without a bed or bedclothes, endures biting vermin and fleas, as well as having to labour hard to bring water and firewood to the poor woman's home and beg for their food.

Margery's accounts continue by sharing some of the most explicit of her visions and revelations. First, she details her vision of her own marriage to Christ in Heaven, witnessed by the Father, the Holy Ghost, the Virgin and a host of saints. She describes how, in a mystical ceremony, Christ accepts her as his wedded wife, 'for fairer, for fouler, for richer, for poorer, provided that you are humble and meek in doing what I command you to do'.[10] Her visions go so far as to include the instruction by Christ that He and she, just as any other husband and wife, should be on 'homely terms' and lie with one another in her bed and that she should kiss him.

Margery arrived back in Bristol in about 1415 where she languished unwell throughout the winter, but resolved to leave on a new pilgrimage in the spring of 1417, this time to the shrine of St James in Spain. Her departure from the port of Bristol was unfortunately timed, since Henry V was then requisitioning ships for his second expedition to France in the same year. Hence she was forced to wait six weeks there before she could set off. Such unforeseen delays were a not uncommon occurrence for pilgrims, though they were not always for political reasons. She eventually arrived at Santiago de Compostela, where she stayed for two weeks. By the time of her return, her account speaks of pain and illness in her head and in her back, which obviously caused great discomfort. Seemingly, over the next eight years, her condition also exacerbated her pious outbursts in church, so much so that the priests no longer gave her communion in front of the rest of the congregation, but in a private chapel, out of earshot! Although Margery had successfully journeyed to the three most esteemed pilgrimage sites – Jerusalem, Rome and Santiago de Compostela – she was to continue on her pilgrimages with unabated enthusiasm and energy.

Despite Margery Kempe's obvious intention to further her spiritual knowledge and commend herself to God, her religious hysteria has caused her to be remembered as a volatile eccentric rather than a saint. This is somewhat unfortunate given Margery's unceasing efforts to promote herself as a true visionary mystic, closely modelling herself as she did on venerable figures such as St Bridget, Mary d'Oignies and Elizabeth of Hungary. Her authenticity and orthodoxy were questioned by many, and her histrionic displays of religious zeal appear only to have undermined her spiritual fervour in the eyes of others. Instead of being held up as exemplary, as were Paula and Egeria, she was most often considered to be the 'poor creature' she describes herself, credited only by a minority who believed her unfortunate disposition to be truly the manifestation of the workings of God.

Some modern critics have accused Margery Kempe of carrying a 'monumental ego' and of lacking the humility that would normally have granted women of her kind a sainthood. However, saint or not, and aside from some perhaps unappealing traits, Margery Kempe bravely shares a raw, personal account of her spiritual journey with total candour. The resulting autobiography is of great significance and value to the modern historian and reader. Rarely, if ever, is such a privileged insight into the life, aspirations and hardships of a medieval woman expressed so fervently in other surviving texts.

FIVE

Chaucer's Leading Ladies – The Wife of Bath and the Prioress

She koulde muchel of wandringe by the weye
Gat-tothed was she, soothly for to seye.[1]

The Wife of Bath is perhaps the most famous of Chaucer's *Canterbury Tales* characters. Provocative, chatty and vivacious, she is embellished with physical features that match her flamboyant nature. She is of a ruddy, outdoors complexion, there is a large gap between her front teeth (believed to indicate a voracious sexual appetite) and she speaks shrilly on account of her partial deafness. She is not someone designed to go unnoticed! While she is the fictional antithesis of such real-life pilgrims as Margery Kempe or St Bridget, with both of whom Chaucer and his audience would have been familiar, it is no coincidence that the Wife's pilgrimage itinerary so closely matches theirs.

Nonetheless, the pilgrimage repertoire of Alison, Wife of Bath, is impressive, with visits to Jerusalem (three times), Rome, Boulogne, Santiago de Compostela and Cologne. Such a record would normally have been the sign of the truly devout, although three visits to the Holy Land might have been considered excessive and, besides, the Wife of Bath was one of pilgrimage's merrymakers. A tough and compulsive traveller, a perpetual pilgrim for reasons of personal gain and pleasure rather than spiritual fulfilment, she was the type of woman whom critics held up as an example of why women should be forbidden to go on pilgrimage at all. She has been married five times and dabbles in 'remedies of love' – presumably anything from potions to induce abortion, to enhance sex drive or performance, or even to cause one to fall in love – or lust.

Alison is exuberant and flamboyant. In her parish she is sure to be the one who presents the most lavish gifts to the priest just to impress, her stockings are of 'fyn scarlet reed' (an expensive colour to produce in the Middle Ages and hence worn mostly by the nobility), her wimple is carefully arranged and she wears a conspicuously large-brimmed hat, as broad as a shield. Her pointed spurs are perhaps an allusion to the sharper, more aggressive aspect of her nature, particularly where her husbands were concerned. Her primary interest is in men and marriage and her Prologue and Tale reflect this, with unexpurgated accounts of her own extensive experience of both. She argues provocatively that while virginity is a fine thing, it is not for everyone and indeed there is nothing in the Bible to enforce it. Set against the backdrop of contemporary misogyny and the opinion of women as sinful, untrustworthy and, at best, a necessary evil, the Wife champions the woman's cause with common-sense argument, supported by her own informed experience.

Chaucer uses her Prologue and Tale to challenge the widely held ideals of the male and female role, in a way that opposed such contemporary opinion and may well have elicited much vitriol from some of his male audience. He develops a character who is a 'professional' wife as well as a perpetual pilgrim in order to embody views on women, marriage *and* women on pilgrimage in one combustible, unashamedly outspoken mouthpiece that is the Wife. He creates a character that runs in the face of medieval convention: she chooses not only to ignore the counsel of the Church that women be chaste, but openly and publicly disagrees with it; she also elects to marry again after being widowed, also against the advice of the Church. Such controversial views and behaviour could not be convincingly portrayed by anyone other than the outrageous, fast-talking Wife, who confidently delivers her opinions in amplified tones to the entire company.

The Wife's favourite themes are the state of marriage and women's place *within* marriage and the home, particularly their desire for control over the household and mastery over their husbands, indeed this becomes the overriding theme of her tale.

Chaucer uses the Wife to play Devil's advocate and subvert the status quo in matters between the sexes. Her views and persona are in blatant contrast to the role of woman as subservient wife. The Wife of Bath is a rare example of a wife exerting power over men in order to show husbands that the wife is really boss. As might be expected, the Wife's secret weapon is often sex, which she advocates rationing, Lysistrata style:

> I wolde no lenger in the bed abide,
> If that I felte his arm over my side,
> Til he had maad his raunson unto me;
> Thanne wolde I suffer him do his nicetee.[2]

Chaucer draws much of his anti-female invective from two early sources, the epistle of Valerius (late first century AD) on not taking a wife, and a work on the state of marriage by Theophrastus (fourth century BC). These works promoted such views as it is better to make your home with a lion or a dragon than with a nagging woman, and that it is preferable to hide in the attic than live in a house with a bad-tempered woman! The Wife's Prologue also pays attention to the issue of husbands' reservations about their wives setting off on travels:

> That ilke proverbe of Ecclesiaste
> Where he comandeth, and forbedeth faste,
> Man shal nat suffer his wyf go roule aboute [gad about].[3]

Any man that

> . . . suffreth his wyf to go seken halwes [to go on pilgrimages],
> Is worthy to been hanged on the galwes [gallows]![4]

The theme of the Wife's tale would have been familiar to Chaucer's fourteenth-century audience; he has preserved the essence of the original while adding a few embellishments of his own. His story tells of a knight of King Arthur's Table who rapes an innocent young maiden. The law demands his death, but the Queen asserts her power over King Arthur, succeeding in persuading him to spare the knight's life and instead allow her to decide his fate. The Queen sets the knight a task. She sends him on a quest to uncover what it is that women most desire. She grants him a year and a day in which to unravel the mystery, otherwise his neck will meet the axe. Through this assertion of her power, the Queen controls the situation, dominating her husband the King as well as the guilty knight.

The knight duly sets out, and knocks at several doors in order to find the answer, only to discover that women desire a whole host of different things:

> Somme seyde women loven best richesse,
> Somme seyde honour, some seyde jolinesse,
> Somme riche array, somme seyden lust abedde,
> And oftetime to be widwe and wedde.[5]

In a witty aside, the Wife tells us that women are said to delight in being considered discreet and steadfast, but in her view that 'is nat worth a rake-stele [handle]'! Women are natural gossips and can keep nothing to themselves, she says. She cites Ovid's tale of Midas and his ass's ears as proof that 'Pardee, we wommen konne no thing hele'.

Disconsolate and so far unsuccessful in his quest, on the appointed day the knight turns for home. However, he comes across an old hag, 'A fouler wight ther may no man devise' (l. 999) with whom he shares the nature of his quest and the old woman promises to help him fulfil his task. In return for her aid, the knight promises her anything she wishes. Their bargain sealed, they head back to King Arthur's court, where the knight delivers his answer:

> Wommen desiren to have sovereinetee
> As well over hir housbond as hir love,
> And for to been in maistrie him above.[6]

Not a single woman at court contested his words and the knight's life is spared, whereupon, and lest he forget, the old woman demands that he fulfil the promise he has made her. In return for her help she requests that he marry her, something to which the knight is forced to consent. Their wedding day passes without joy or festivity and on their wedding night, the knight confesses that he is ashamed of the old woman's looks, advanced years and lowly status.

His bride listens to his objections and promises she can make things appear better if he will hear her out. She then proceeds to lecture him on the quality of 'gentilesse', the quality of nobility, saying that it is not inherent only in those of high birth, 'For gentilesse cometh fro God allone' (l. 1162). Regarding her humble status, she argues that God Himself had chosen to live as a poor man and lists many reasons why poverty might be considered a 'hateful good'. Finally, she argues for the advantages of being married to a lowly, ugly old wife and then asks the knight to make a crucial choice. He must decide whether she should remain 'foul and old', but 'a trewe, humble wyf' to him, or whether she should become 'yong and fair' but the cause of his worldly misery with the traffic of her lovers' t'oing and fro'ing from their front door. The knight responds, 'I put me in youre wise governance', requesting that she choose whichever option she deems best and most honourable for both of them. Triumphantly she answers: 'Thanne have I got of yow maistrie' (l. 1236), and requests that he kiss her. The old woman transforms at his kisses, shedding her years and taking on such a fairness of face that 'His herte bathed in a bath of blisse'. The Wife here ends her tale with a parting shot – that God send all women fine young husbands who keep their wives happy, and a plague on those who do not!

Unlike the extrovert and overpowering Wife of Bath, the character of the Prioress is apparently her genteel antithesis, if also presenting something of a conundrum. The oddest fact is that she is among Chaucer's pilgrims in the first place for the contemporary Church normally required strict confinement of nuns to the cloister. Both Chaucer and his audience would have known of Pope Boniface VIII's bull of 1298, the *Pericoloso* formalising this restriction on nuns' freedom of movement.

To the medieval ear, the Prioress's name, Madame Eglentyne, would immediately have conjured up ideas of love, mercy and holiness as one of the flowers and symbols of the Virgin Mary. However, in an ironic twist Chaucer has chosen a name deliberately at odds with the Prioress's character. While in the lines of the General Prologue she appears to be the respectable woman in holy orders whom we would expect, Chaucer's text gradually reveals someone rather different, his most illuminating piece of information coming in the last line of our introduction to her in the General Prologue:

> And theron heng a brooch of gold full sheene,
> On which ther was first write a crowned A,
> And after *Amor vincit omnia*.[7]

While it was not unheard of for a nun to wear a brooch with her rosary, hers seems to serve as worldy adornment rather than spiritual appendage. Moreover, its inscription is questionable. Rather than carrying an excerpt from Scripture, it bears a mantra of courtly and profane love, 'Love conquers all'. As a nun, Madame Eglentyne should know nothing of human or physical love.

Another tell-tale element in her dress is the care with which her wimple is arranged. Far from being a modest item of attire, hers has been 'Full semely . . . pinched' or pleated and pushed unnaturally high in accordance with the fashion of the day so as to reveal a 'fair forheed . . . almost a spanne brood' (ll. 154–5). It seems that much of the Prioress's thought is concerned with show and appearance in a way reminiscent of the 'Ywimpled well' Wife of Bath, except that this is particularly ill advised for a woman in holy orders out in public, whose morals and modesty should have been her primary concern.

Chaucer tempers her vanity with two qualities more appropriate to the Prioress's calling, traits that initially appear to tie in rather better with the pilgrimage ideal, for he describes her as 'so charitable and so pitous' that she was prone to weep. However, these are not the theatrical weepings of Margery Kempe at the Holy Sepulchre. Chaucer reveals that the Prioress's charity and pity were reserved for such instances as a mouse being caught in a trap, or were roused by any ill that might befall the small dogs that she indulges. Some critics have detected an underlying sadness in the Prioress's character: a woman dissatisfied with her religious lot and who perhaps regrets the missed opportunity for earthly love or bearing children, the latter manifested in her maternal coddling of her dogs. It is interesting that just over a decade before Chaucer's *Tales*, the knight, Geoffrey de la Tour-Landry had written a book of moral precepts for his daughters in order to make them desirable as wives and teach them the courtesies expected of noblewomen. In one of his exempla, he relates the tale of a woman who 'gaf the flesshe to her honndes' noting that she does so at the expense of those suffering from hunger. The tale is contrived as an incentive to the performance of good works for the poor, the hungry and those in need. The woman is brought to her senses by means of a rather sinister vision on her sick bed, in which two dogs approach her bed and lick her lips with their tongues, making her mouth as 'black as a Cole'. Certainly in the case of the Prioress, the concern for the poor and needy should have been uppermost, but the unseemly indulgence of her dogs appears to reflect a profound desire for motherhood rather than for any religious calling. One might even draw a parallel between the special diet of tender meats and bread softened with milk she bestows on her hounds with those recommended for infants in the Middle Ages.

In the Prologue to her Tale, the Prioress makes particular reference to children as divine and precious beings, 'from the mouths of children Thy bounty Is hymned, yea, even sucklings at the breast, Do sometimes Thy laudation manifest'. She also draws several parallels between herself and the Virgin Mary, in the Virgin's role as divine intermediary in matters of fertility, conception and motherhood, referring to her frequently as 'Cristes moder', emphasising Mary's holy and maternal function while underscoring her own religious status. Her Prologue and Tale are also deeply intertwined with the theme of the Virgin and her affiliated devotion. Moreover, the Prioress seems determined to portray herself as something much greater than the modest and introspective nun she should have been. All of which contribute to a persona that has been described by one scholar as one of 'delicious ambiguity'.[8]

We learn too that the Prioress exhibits a flair for the social niceties, also not befitting a cloistered nun. She is described as entertaining and pleasant and as feigning courtly behaviour,

> and peyned hire to countrefeite cheere
> Of courte, and to been estatlich of manere[9]

After the fashion of courtly ladies with refined table manners, the Prioress reaches delicately for her food, manages not to drop any of it between mouth and table, leaves no residue on the side of her cup or on her lips when she drinks and, miraculously, given the inevitable perils of eating from a bread trencher designed to soak up the fatty juices, manages not to get her fingers dirty. She is also described as speaking French:

> ful faire and fetisly [elegantly],
> After the scole of Stratford atte Bowe,
> For Frenssh of Parys was to hire unknowe.[10]

This is another indication by Chaucer of the Prioress's courtly affectations, but hers is schoolbook French, not derived through any association with Paris or from having been to France; it is merely another display of inappropriate and showy elegance. Madame Eglantyne also associates herself with 'Seynte Loy', or St Faith, at the centre of a cult based in Conques, France. The Prioress's choice is described by one critic as 'the most elegant and courtly saint in the calendar, one thoroughly representative of feminine tastes which she preserved in spite of her devotion to religion . . .'.[11]

Chaucer's is a sardonic portrayal of a woman of affected airs, whose quirky imitation of aristocratic manners reveals her uneasy association with the true vocation of a nun. Such endeavours to behave above and outside of her allotted station and religious vocation imply that the Prioress's thoughts have strayed from the spiritual path; they also bring to mind the warnings voiced by Pope Boniface VIII, Caesarius of Arles (*c*. AD 468–470 to 542)[12] and others on the dangers of worldly temptation for the innocent. The Prioress epitomises the very traps they seek to forestall. Her spirit is moved not by the apprehension of God, but by the enjoyment of good company, by personal vanity, in fine attire and jewellery, and her excessive affection for her dogs, all of which she indulges under the pretext of pilgrimage, wearing the nun's habitual attire, but stretching the boundaries of ecclesiastical behaviour and dress as far as she can.

While the Prioress shows excessive tenderness towards her dogs, her feelings towards people are portrayed as the exact opposite. Her tale contains alarming elements of violence and anti-Semitism. Along with her penchant for fashionable jewellery, courtly ideals and behaviour, it seems that she has also adopted the unappealing and strongly anti-Semitic sentiment rampant at the time. Through her thin veneer of piety, she relates her tale of the murder of an innocent young boy. With due biblical reference she tells of his murder at the hands of Jews, but her quotations from Psalm 7 are carefully chosen for they are those used in the Mass for the Feast of the Holy Innocents, and so serve as an unequivocal reminder of the murder of small children on the orders of Herod the Great in his attempt to eradicate the Son of God.

Her tale was in fact a popular subject for contemporary ballads. Generally known as the 'Tale of the Chorister' it would have been familiar to Chaucer's audience. A young schoolboy learns a difficult Latin hymn in praise of the Virgin Mary because of his own deep devotion to her. Each day, the young boy has to pass through the Jewish ghetto to get to and from school and would sing his new hymn. One day, however, a group of Jews take offence at the song, interpreting its words as an insult, and have an assassin slit the boy's throat and throw his body into a pit. What follows is the desperate search by the child's widowed mother for her missing son. She runs through the streets and the ghetto asking if anyone has seen her son, but the Jews refuse to help her. Eventually, she recovers his body, which is then carried to the abbey. In an allusion to numerous miracle stories expounded at shrines across Europe, in spite of his cut throat the young boy is still able to sing his hymn to which the townsfolk are compellingly drawn. At his final resting place, he is able to speak before he is buried because of a pearl that his precious Virgin has placed on his tongue. The tale ends on this poignant note with the burial of the child and the Prioress's curse on the Jewish perpetrators of the crime.

Chaucer's tales were set against the social backdrop of anti-Semitism that was prevalent in England as elsewhere in Europe and as such the theme of the Prioress's tale would have struck a chord with her fellow pilgrims and Chaucer's audience. In 1290, the Jews had been expelled from England by Edward I. The popular literature of Chaucer's age in the fourteenth century became ever more imbued with anti-Semitic themes, with the Jews perceived as a malevolent race, or agents of the Devil. The Prioress's tale represents a blood libel story, an articulation of the belief that the Jews were wont to kidnap and murder young children as part of their Passover ritual. Other stories concerning the murder of young children by Jews were also in circulation. It even seems that such stories incited so much hatred in the medieval Christian imagination that Popes Clement V, Innocent III, Innocent IV and Gregory X all went some way to try and prevent their dissemination, for fear of the violence they provoked.[13] It is precisely such a rendering of the story as the Prioress's that might have provoked violent 'reprisals' for she embellishes many of the details and delivers a far bloodier and more violent version of the tale to her listeners. The violence of the punishment to be meted out to the Jews is also unequalled in other versions of the story. The underlying message of her narration, one which she reinforces with calculated emotion, is the perceived sin and guilt of the Jews as the executioners of Christ. The Prioress exhibits a disquieting satisfaction in the cursing and punishment of the Jewish protagonists, introducing them as hateful to Christ and those who are His own and concluding with the punishment: 'Yvele shal have that yvele wol deserve' – 'evil shall have what evil does deserve'; the Jews were dragged behind wild horses and afterwards hung. She shows an alarmingly unmerciful, vindictive nature in her rendering of the tale and it is received with silence by her fellow pilgrims at its end. Such harsh and bloodthirsty sentiments seem at odds with her refined airs and concern for her animals. Are we to suppose that she was unaware of the bigoted, unmerciful persona she adopts in her re-telling of the story, or is Chaucer allowing the true nature of her anti-Semitism to surface for the purposes of her rhetoric and the stirring of her audience's response?

The development of the Prioress and Wife of Bath's characters in their Prologues and Tales is employed by Chaucer as a vehicle for his social commentary. Both are far from conventional portrayals: the wayward, over-experienced Wife on pilgrimage, unescorted by a spouse in the same party as the corrupted innocence of the Prioress out of the safety of her cloister. Both manifest some highly unappealing traits that would have registered with Chaucer's audience as ironic commentary. While he chooses popular and recognisable characters, from the devious Pardoner to the avaricious Monk, he perhaps intended to be most distasteful the existence of such unappealing traits in women, medieval society's vulnerable sex, its mothers, carers and nurturers.

The devious behaviour, lasciviousness and misplaced devotions of his female characters – a woman that should have been at home with her husband, or at least accompanied by him, and a nun who would have done better never to have left her cloister – would have roused the interest of his audience as a literary critique of some of the vices of women that prevailed in contemporary commentary. He incorporates contemporary social criticism of women on pilgrimage, drawing on early texts and adding his own twist of irony and humour, so that while delivering a thoroughly enjoyable résumé of each of his pilgrim's attributes and qualities, we are also meant to appreciate his penetrating exposé of the current social climate.

SIX

The Holy, the Mystic and the Cloistered

Ther was also a Nonne, a Prioresse,
That of hir smylyng was ful symple and coy;
Hire gretteste ooth was but by Seinte Loy.[1]

ocumentary evidence suggests that pilgrimage activity among women had begun as early as the fourth century, and it seems that criticism was swift to follow. Particular concern was expressed at the notion that nuns, who had vowed themselves to religious service within the convent, should uproot themselves and travel overseas on pilgrimage, thus 'displacing' themselves from the convent and laying themselves in harm's way. In his advice to Eadburga, an English abbess, Pope Boniface had found himself in something of a quandary. On the one hand a nun's place was in her cloister, but on the other she may find solace by visiting the holy shrines in Rome. He therefore declined to commit himself to advising Eadburga either way. However, another letter reveals that Eadburga did in fact make her pilgrimage to Rome and that she managed to meet Boniface there.

The Pope was concerned that the safety and honour of women and nuns on pilgrimage would be put at risk. His letter to Archbishop Cuthbert of Canterbury in the middle of the eighth century was an effort to curb the numbers of Englishwomen and nuns arriving in Rome: 'A great part of them perish and few keep their virtue. There are very few towns in Lombardy or Frankland or Gaul where there is not a courtesan or harlot of English stock. . . .'[2] The Synod of Friuli (*c.* 795) actually legislated against nuns going on pilgrimage:

And at no time whatsoever shall it be permitted to any abbess or nun to go to Rome or to tour other holy places, if Satan should transform himself into an angel of light and suggest it to them as if for the purpose of prayer. No one is so obtuse or stupid as to be unaware how irreligious and reprehensible it is [for them] to have dealings with men on account of the necessities of travel. . .[3]

If the usual reasons for preventing women and nuns in particular from embarking on pilgrimage were concerns for their safety, such concern was grounded in fact. In addition to the normal dangers such as robbery and illness, women faced the hazard of sexual threat – or temptation. The nun leaving the safe environment of her convent might well have found herself less experienced in the ways of the world than the village or town womenfolk, who would have been accustomed to wider social interaction and rather more freedom of movement. Chaucer makes a parallel statement when he comments of the Monk, 'Is likned til a fissh that is waterlees – This is to seyn, a monk out of his cloistre.'[4]

Perhaps the best known instance of a pilgrim group running into trouble was an expedition to Jerusalem under the Bishop of Bamberg in 1064–5. He led a party of clergy and laymen that was harassed and assaulted by the 'pagans' of the Holy Land who stole from them and at whose hands they lost several members of their group. The pilgrims were pursued on horseback by the 'Enemies of Christ'. The death of an abbess among their number, received particular attention:

> [a] noble abbess, fair of form and devout of mind, who had abandoned the care of the sisters entrusted to her and against all the advice of wiser heads had subjected herself to the dangers of this pilgrimage. She was captured by the pagans, and in the sight of everybody, raped by the shameless ones for so long that at last, to the disgrace of all Christians, she breathed her last.[5]

The incident is much recounted as a cautionary tale for women in holy orders that they might be inclined rather to remain in the safety and sanctity of the cloister than to lay themselves open to such potential horrors. It states unambiguously that the abbess had ignored the advice and concerns of her sisters in undertaking the pilgrimage and that, clearly, they had been right in advising her not to go. While the entire party came under attack, more significant here is the gender-specific danger such a journey might entail for a woman, however 'devout of mind' – rape and death at pagan hands.

Towards the close of the eleventh century, with the First Crusade in 1095, it appears that some cloistered monks and nuns saw an opportunity for pilgrimage that would be difficult to gainsay in terms of its efficacy and value. Brother Felix Fabri tells us that 'many nuns broke the bonds of their obedience without leave or licence'.[6]

By the thirteenth century, Pope Innocent III was particularly concerned at the problem of the cloistered religious overstepping the bounds of Church discipline, particularly nuns attempting to transcend their prescribed canonical authority. Writing in 1202, he states that he was appalled to hear that abbesses were blessing their nuns, hearing their confessions, reading the gospel and presuming to preach in public. He completely forbade this 'absurdity' since 'even though the most blessed Virgin Mary was more worthy and more excellent than all of the apostles, yet not to her, but to them the Lord handed over the keys to the kingdom of heaven'.[7] Based on his teaching, canonists consistently forbade the performance by women of any duty that might belong to the power of the keys. Writing in the thirteenth century, the Dominican Raymund of Peñaforte concluded, 'Hence even an abbess, however learned, holy or religious, is not able to preach, nor to bless, nor to excommunicate, nor to absolve, nor to give penance, nor to judge, nor to exercise the office of any order.'[8]

A legatine council held at York in June 1195 by Archbishop Hubert Walter had placed further restrictions on the cloistered stating that monks, canons and nuns should be forbidden to undertake pilgrimage; particular reference was made to nuns with the dictat that they should never be allowed to leave the convent unless under supervision and in the company of their superiors:

> The profession of religious holiness requires that monks and canons regular and nuns live religiously and according to rule. So therefore as to deprive them of the opportunity of wandering about, we forbid them to . . . undertake pilgrimages, to leave the monastery without definite and reasonable cause, or to go out without the company of someone whose character is beyond doubt. With respect to nuns especially, we add that they must not leave the enclosure of the convent except in the company of the abbess or prioress.[9]

While such rules might be open to laxer interpretations certainly there were now numerous obstacles to and diverging opinions of pilgrimage activity with which the cloistered had to contend if they were to enjoy any freedom of movement. A letter of the mid-fourteenth century from Pope Clement VI to Philip VI of France suggests that in addition, nuns now found themselves caught up in a situation whereby they could not receive the Jubilee indulgence from the seven pilgrimage churches of Rome *unless* they made a pilgrimage and appeared there in person. A request that enclosed nuns, along with those who were sick or frail, unable to visit the churches be granted the indulgence without physically visiting the places met with outright refusal: 'no one, of whatever status, condition, religious order or rank, no matter with what dignity they be invested, may obtain this indulgence except by personally visiting the basilicas . . .'.[10]

The medieval sentiment that everyone should remain where life had placed them and that in this way nuns should stay within the cloister hardly worked in the nuns' favour with regard to pilgrimage. The argument that pilgrimage by the cloistered was a deviation from their avowed path within the confines of their religious houses was to have a long future: 'It is necessary that those who make profession in a particular place must take up the cross of the Lord, and follow the Lord, in that place, and not seek a foreign burial ground.' However, a chronicle for 1300 recounts that many pilgrims from all over Christendom, 'men, women, clerks, laymen, religious male and female, and nuns' alike went to Rome in this the first Jubilee year. The chronicle emphasised the importance and impact that the Jubilee in Rome had on the pilgrimage industry and the apparently infinite numbers of pilgrims who arrived to receive their indulgences at the basilicas of Rome:

> barons, knights and great ladies, and others without number of both sexes and every condition, status, order and dignity. . . . Every day it seemed as if a general army was passing every hour along the strata Claudia, both in the city and outside it. . . .[11]

While monks appeared to enjoy a greater degree of freedom than nuns in this matter, both were essentially still under the jurisdiction of their ecclesiastical superiors. Monks might also find themselves confronted with similar arguments against their wish to go on pilgrimage. The Canons of Hereford took the interesting step of devising a kind of sabbatical system to control the numbers and absence of those undertaking pilgrimage within their orders.

Subjects were restricted to only one overseas pilgrimage in their lifetime. Equally, time limits were imposed on their pilgrimages: three weeks for those within England, four months for Rome or Santiago and a year for Jerusalem.[12] A letter written by the Abbot of Vendôme to Abbot Odo in the eleventh century with regard to the latter's seeming intention to leave the monastery for the Holy Land expresses contemporary misgivings about the cloistered on pilgrimage in no uncertain terms:

> There is an unpleasant rumour in circulation, which has come to our ears that you have it in mind to return to Jerusalem. To have seen Jerusalem once should suffice you; and if you have never seen it, no diabolical calumny could have arisen against you on this account, nor would you require God's forgiveness. The bond of the monastic profession cannot be maintained by going to Jerusalem, only violated.[13]

In the case of a Dominican Friar from Ulm, Felix Fabri, a second journey to the Holy Land was actually made, his reason being that he had derived such enjoyment from the first! It seems highly likely that any woman in holy orders would have had to struggle hard to obtain licence for the undertaking of a second pilgrimage to the same site. Perhaps, though, the concerns voiced by Fabri before he set off on his first voyage to the Holy Land mirror the sentiments of all in cloistered orders who sought to go on pilgrimage:

> it was a serious matter for me to ask leave for so long and so unusual a wandering, and it appeared to be almost impossible for me to obtain it. Nor could I form any idea of how I should raise the money for such an expensive journey.[14]

Brother Fabri's enthusiasm for a return pilgrimage to the Holy Land was coupled with anxiety as to the probable reception his request would elicit from his superiors:

I did not dare to reveal to my Father in God my scheme for returning to Jerusalem, lest I might trouble his spirit, and lest both he and others when they heard it might be scandalized at me, judging me to be light-minded and impatient of the quiet of the cloister, or perhaps suffering from temptations of the devil, or guilty of the sin of idle curiosity, or moved by frivolity. So I remained undecided, and made no sign of what I felt, save that when questioned about Jerusalem and the Holy Land, I could not speak without sighing. . . .[15]

The fact that pilgrimage continued to be undertaken by cloistered men and women alike shows not only the powerful draw the enterprise exercised and the magnetism of the indulgence in a Jubilee year, but also that no sufficiently stringent rules were imposed to eliminate completely the possibility of pilgrimage by nuns. However, opposition and recommendation against its practice by the cloistered did have a profound effect on the numbers of nuns to be found on pilgrimage. Pope Boniface VIII's bull *Pericoloso* (1298) mentioned earlier had underscored the need to keep nuns in the cloister and away from the normal routine and business of the outside world. While it did not mention pilgrimage directly, it was readily accepted by many that this was what was being implied.

The earliest such rules written specifically for women had been compiled in the sixth century by Caesarius of Arles in his 'Rules for Nuns' (*Regula ad Moniales*) and there are clear similarities with *Pericoloso*'s stipulations. Caesarius had also written a rule for monks, but it was that for nuns which specified the maintenance of their enclosure.

Among those listed as having permission granted by Edward III for the second Jubilee of 1350, there is only one nun. Her name was Matilda Montague. As it was, Matilda was no ordinary nun, for she had been born into a privileged and prosperous family of distinction. It seems that in Matilda's case, her family enjoyed royal favour, a fact that may have helped secure her permission to travel to Rome as a nun in the Jubilee year.

Boniface's assertion of the benefits of enforced enclosure reflect the preoccupation of the times: 'the nuns . . . wholly separated from the public and worldly gaze, and occasions for lasciviousness having been removed, may most diligently safeguard their hearts and bodies in complete chastity'.[16] Of course the concept of removing women and nuns from potential temptation was tied in to the common belief that, being inherently weak, they were less able to resist sexual temptation. In a letter from the theologian Peter Abelard to the cloistered abbess Heloise he counsels:

Solitude is indeed all the more necessary for your woman's frailty, in as much as for our part we are less attacked by the conflicts of carnal temptations and less likely to stray towards bodily things through the senses. . . .[17]

English bishops were all too ready to cite compliance with Boniface's bull as a means of enforcing their own, parochial measures to curtail nuns' freedom, applying *Pericoloso*'s strictures directly to pilgrimage activity. In 1318, the Archbishop of York made an imaginative attempt to dissuade the nuns from foreign travel. Those nuns who had already vowed to take pilgrimage were instead to recite a number of psalters commensurate with the number of days it would have taken them to undergo their pilgrimage. The nuns responded by arguing that a vow made could not be revoked hence it would be wrong for them not to act on it. In 1344, Bishop Hamo de Hethe of Rochester sought to curb the pilgrimage activities of the nuns of Malling. He attempted to rein them in to stop them wandering about the countryside visiting their friends on the pretext of pilgrimage. In the event, he exacted an oath from their abbess to ensure that such freedoms were withdrawn.

Chaucer uses the character of his Prioress to illustrate contemporary concerns about the cloistered on pilgrimage. His audience would have immediately been struck by the fact of her being on pilgrimage at all. While Chaucer tends to draw a definitive, black-or-white line in the portrayal of his characters as either convention-ally pious or distinctly avaricious or untrustworthy, the Prioress seems to have an uneasy foot in both camps.

By the fourteenth century, concern had extended from the issue of the safety of women in religious orders travelling to foreign lands to include anxieties that such journeys might be used as an opportune excuse for an excursion from the confines of the cloister, even as a kind of foray while still under the auspices of pilgrimage. In 1301, an amazed Archbishop Winchesley had written to the prior and chapter of Canterbury to complain at how many monks appeared to be seeking to visit holy relics 'feigning devotion under the veil of pilgrimage as a result of vows'. He is particularly astonished that such monks travel to the relics at Pontigny and Hereford among other distant shrines when, as he says, Canterbury has its own abundance of relics on their doorstep! He too was concerned at the religious exposing themselves to all manner of temptation and evil when they 'throw aside monastic modesty . . . wandering around the world, embrace impiety, create scandals and make themselves and others, by their pernicious example, less receptive to religious observance'.[18]

However, those women of orders who did manage to take pilgrimages demonstrate that it was possible to transcend the boundaries set by their superiors with the right motives and the right contacts. Mary, daughter of Edward I and a nun at Amesbury in Wiltshire went on several pilgrimages to famous shrines. She was also the Prioress of Clerkenwell, 1331. She accompanied her stepmother, Queen Margaret, on a pilgrimage of thanksgiving for her help during her confinement prior to the birth of her second son. She later accompanied her niece, Elizabeth de Burgh. It was for her that a Dominican friar Nicholas Trevet (Trivet) wrote an Anglo-Norman chronicle of world history in 1334, on which Chaucer's Man of Law's Tale is based. Its protagonist Constance travels throughout Europe and the Middle East:

virtue is her guide;
Meekness in her has humbled tyranny;
She is the mirror of all courtesy;
Her heart's a very shrine of holiness. . . .[19]

Those visionaries and mystics who chose a life of seclusion and celibacy were able to move about or relocate a little more freely, as they existed outside the conventional boundaries of domesticity or the enclosed cloisters of the nunnery. Often we find that women chose such a life when their husbands died and they were widowed. They lived a life of renewed ascetic piety and often chastity. As with the practice of pilgrimage itself, this was a phenomenon that occurred across all levels of medieval society, from the ordinary womenfolk of towns and villages to widows of noble households.

As we saw earlier, Margery Kempe appears to have adopted a similar path later in life although her husband was still alive. She told him that she wished to become chaste again and refused sexual relations with him. As with many of Margery's decisions, this one was taken with passionate determination: 'paying the debt of matrimony was so abominable to her that she would rather, she thought, have eaten and drunk the ooze and muck in the gutter than consent to intercourse . . .'.[20]

Only after a lengthy struggle with her husband that lasted some three or four years does Margery finally get her way and we are told that her husband too took a vow of chastity. She left him and her children behind to take several pilgrimages during which she reported many ecstatic episodes and spiritual revelations. She followed a strict regime of vigils, fasting and wore a penitential hair shirt.

Two of Margery Kempe's guiding lights and inspirations were St Bridget and the mystic Julian of Norwich. Throughout her travels and spiritual journey, Margery constantly sought out the counsel of such mystics and recluses wishing to emulate their purity and piety, as well as effecting similar devoutness, albeit in her case

A view of the city of Jerusalem from the 'advis directif pour faire le passaige d'oultre mer' by Burchard du Mont Sion, *c.* 1455. *(Bibliothèque nationale, Paris/Bridgeman Art Library)*

St Cuthbert, dressed as a bishop, heals a sick child, from *The Life of St Cuthbert* by Bede, late twelfth century, Durham. Yates Thompson, 26, f.62v. *(© The British Library/Heritage-Images)*

A fifteenth-century illustration of two women fighting. MS Hunter 252 f.186r. *(Glasgow University Library/Bridgeman Art Library)*

'The Joys of Marriage'. *Above:* a husband at a souvenir stall for his wife; *below left:* his wife going off on pilgrimage with her lover. *(akg-images/Erich Lessing)*

Right: A fourteenth-century wall painting of a female pilgrim at prayer, Notre Dame Church, Avy-en-Pons, France. *(akg-images/ Jean-Paul Dumontier)*

Queen Isabella of Portugal on pilgrimage, *c.* 1500–25, from the 'Tavoa primeira dos Reyes de Portugal'. Add. 12531, f.96. *(© The British Library/Heritage-Images)*

Suffrages of the Saints. St Catherine with her wheel and St Barbara with her tower, St Margarita, St Apollonia, St Lucia and St Clare in a nun's habit, from the Saluces Hours, Italy, mid-fifteenth century. Add. 27697 fol. 100v. *(© The British Library)*

A noble lady worshipping the Virgin and child. *(Bibliothèque nationale de France)*

St Veronica holding the sudarium of Christ's image, *c.* 1420. *(Alte Pinakothek, Munich/Bridgeman Art Library)*

St Dominic saves drowning pilgrims from the River Garonne, detail from an altarpiece in Barcelona. *(akg-images)*

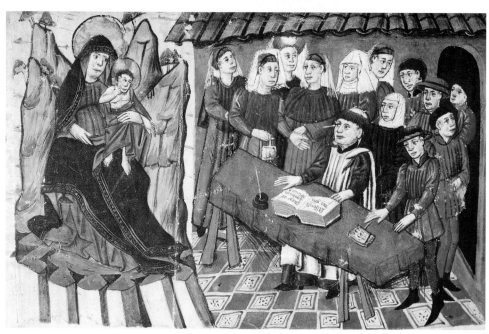

An abbot writing to the monks of the Confraternity of the Virgin of Monserrat. *(© Archivo Iconografico, S.A./CORBIS)*

The Prioress from
Geoffrey Chaucer's
Canterbury Tales,
Ellesmere Manuscript,
1911. *(Private
Collection/Bridgeman
Art Library)*

The Wife of Bath
from Geoffrey
Chaucer's *Canterbury
Tales*, Ellesmere
Manuscript, 1911.
*(Private Collection/
Bridgeman Art
Library)*

St Zita from the Hastings Hours, Flemish, 1483. Add. 54782, f.66v. *(akg-images/British Library)*

An illustration of a pilgrim being attacked and robbed from 'Le Pélerinage de la vie humaine' by Gilliame de Deguilleville, MS Français 823. *(akg-images/VISIOARS)*

this was rather theatrically expressed. Her visions and ecstasies are also reminiscent of those recounted by her heroine, Bridget of Sweden. In order to validate and endorse her mystical episodes for her audience, Margery frequently exploits the name of Bridget in her relation of events, likening herself to a second daughter of Christ and sister to Bridget. She claims that the Lord tells her: 'For in truth I tell you, just as I spoke to St Bridget, just so I speak to you, daughter, and I tell you that every word written in Bridget's book is true, and through you shall be recognised as truth indeed.'[21]

There were, too, mystics who began their careers at a young age, enjoying the freedom of pilgrimage as a vehicle for furthering their spiritual knowledge, as well as maintaining a programme of penance, contemplation and the dissemination of their own personal doctrine.

Ursulina was a fourteenth-century virgin and visionary from Parma in Italy in whose life the established pattern of miracles, visions and ecstasies was played out. On one notable occasion, she received divine guidance urging her to travel to Avignon. During this time the Great Western Schism was the source of much anxiety within the Church. Just as St Bridget, who had also felt very strongly about the return of the Pope to Rome, Ursulina felt guided to visit the antipope Clement VII in Avignon in order to try and convince him to relinquish his power. She then travelled on to Rome to meet Pope Boniface IX.

While she failed in her undertaking, it is of particular interest here that Ursulina involved herself in the reversal of a political situation for she was still only in her teens; and the cause was one that St Bridget had also tried to remedy through her own works, as did her daughter Catherine after her. This episode serves to illustrate the demonstrably greater freedom of movement such women enjoyed as recognised and, in the case of Bridget, revered mystics and visionaries. While women were forbidden to preach and there was no role assigned for them in socio-political matters, these women achieved recognition in their self-appointed vocations as God's messengers, intermediaries, even ambassadors. While most women without birth or connections to royalty would not have managed to gain an audience with the Pope, these women were, to an extent, listened to, even if their influence and powers of persuasion were insufficient to achieve their goal. From Rome Ursulina undertook a pilgrimage to the Holy Land before returning to Parma.

As with the reports of miraculous cures and events at shrines across Europe, seldom was there any concrete proof that the beneficiary had really been the recipient of divine intercession through a particular saint. Equally, there is little way of either authenticating or disproving the visions and revelations of such self-proclaimed mystics. It was not within the medieval pysche's belief system to reject or deny such women, although again, as with many miracles, the revelations and visions of such later canonised saints as Bridget did eventually come under the scrutiny of Church officials.

Such women had set themselves apart from society, stepping outside their conventional role and existing instead as self-appointed vassals of God's holy work. Their lives of penitence, chastity, seclusion and inner reflection were considered conducive to the conveying of such divine counsel. For the enclosed nun, her life of celibacy and piety within the confines of the cloister might also make her a fitting subject for guided acts of piety and writings, but the anchorite or visionary existing in the world outside had the opportunity for a broader canvas on which to display divine inspiration. It was in this way, however, that such women might also find themselves under attack. For example, in what was probably a misguided attempt to promote herself as the bride of Christ, Margery Kempe was apprehended in Canterbury and accused of being a heretic. Equally, Ursulina came to be accused of dabbling in sorcery.

Another mystic and visionary was Bona of Pisa (1156–1207), of whom it is recounted that she experienced visual ecstasies from a very early age during which she was blessed by St James the Great of Santiago de Compostela. By the age of ten she had vowed herself to

the Augustinian rule. At fourteen she was travelling to the Holy
Land on pilgrimage, purportedly to see her father who was on
crusade. She also followed the exact path of Jesus's ministry,
beginning at the River Jordan and ending at Calvary. On her way
home, she was captured and imprisoned by Muslim pirates while
crossing the Mediterranean, but was eventually rescued and
ransomed by some merchants from her home town. Thereafter she
travelled to Rome as a pilgrim and to Santiago de Compostela
several times, leading other pilgrims. It was on the route to Santiago
de Compostela that she received recognition as an official pilgrim
guide under the auspices of the Knights of St James. Bona continued
her life of piety and penitence and under the guided instruction of
St James, built the church of San Jacopo di Podio just north of her
home city of Pisa. She is also said to have offered up her own body
in sacrifice when the River Arno at Pisa threatened to flood its
banks.

Fifty years after Bona's death, her Life was written in the form of
a collection of anecdotes by those who had known her or who had
been the recipient of miraculous cures through her divine
intercession. It begins with the remarkable story of her childhood
and her request to join the Augustinian sisters of St Martin at the
age of ten. The miracles associated with her are said to have begun
when she was still a child. Her Life recounts how when travelling
home one day after running an errand for her mother, she bowed
and crossed herself at the image of Christ outside the Church of the
Holy Sepulchre. The image was said to have responded by bowing
and extending a hand to Bona. On another occasion the image was
said to have breathed into her mouth, imparting to her speech and
actions the goodness of the Holy Spirit.

When she was thirteen, Bona reported a visitation from Christ
himself, disguised as a pilgrim. Her mother had come to see her in
the solitary cell where she lived out her frugal existence. The
stranger, for such he appeared to Bona's mother, told her that he had
news that her estranged husband was safe and well. Bona's father

had left their home in Pisa when his daughter was three, travelling to the Holy Land where he began a new family. Certain that their visitor had been Christ Himself, Bona set out on a journey to find her father and so embarked upon what became a life of perpetual pilgrimage.

At the end of her life, Bona was miraculously transported one final time on a pilgrimage to Santiago de Compostela by her own patron, St James, and brought back home again. Today Bona is considered the patron saint of couriers, guides, pilgrims, flight attendants and all travellers.

Belief systems do, however, change with time and we see a very different reception accorded to Elizabeth Barton, a sixteenth-century nun of Kent who lived near to the major pilgrimage centre of Canterbury. Like Bridget and Bona, Elizabeth began her career as a visionary mystic at an early age, espousing political causes, challenging the status quo, spreading Catholic doctrine, political campaigns and canvassing for them at the feet of kings and popes. However, Elizabeth Barton, the 'holy maid of Kent' or 'mad nun of Kent' as she was also known, took the somewhat audacious step in support of Holy Mother Church of challenging King Henry VIII's proposed divorce from Catherine of Aragon. She challenged him 'in the name and by the authority of God', herself petitioned both the Pope and Wolsey and so made herself a formidable opponent to the King in his 'great matter'.

Her prophecies and visions were endorsed after the deliberations of three monks sent to assess her by the Archbishop of Canterbury himself, and she became a Benedictine nun. Her sanctity was thus authenticated and the fame of her visionary prophecy began to spread. For the purposes of Henry VIII's agenda, however, Elizabeth Barton constituted an obstacle with which he must dispense. She was executed at Tyburn in 1534, taking with her a string of sympathisers.

Such women mystics and pilgrims as Bona, St Bridget and the Nun of Kent represent a select minority of women who enjoyed a greater degree of freedom and movement within medieval society than their lay sisters. If their holiness became sufficiently widely recognised, they might even be granted audiences with the likes of kings and popes. However, such empowerment had to be employed wisely if they were to achieve their goals. Had Margery Kempe ever found herself in the presence of king or pope it is likely that her outlandish displays of affective piety would have caused distaste rather than inspired respect. To this day, there is still debate as to whether Elizabeth Barton really was the vessel of divine intuition and prophecy, or whether she was simply an impostor.

By the reign of Henry VIII, opinions regarding the efficacy of pilgrimage had altered, due in part to the inordinate number of purported holy relics that had flooded Europe. The pilgrimage industry was about to undergo a dramatic change. Commentators had come to criticise certain shrines for the behaviour of their pilgrims, with those favoured by women coming in for particular scrutiny, as in the case of the shrine at Walsingham which was the object too of Erasmus' irony. He made disparaging comments about the efficacy of the shrine, saying that 'the church is graceful and elegant; but the Virgin does not occupy it'.[22] The earlier, comparatively halcyon days of pilgrimage enjoyed by Paula, Egeria, Helena and Catherine were over and women's motives, practices and even claims to divinely guided instruction, visions and ecstasies came in for much closer scrutiny. We shall examine the reasons for these changes in the final chapter.

SEVEN

The Royal, the Rich and the Noble

I heard yesterday that a worsted man of Norfolk, that sold worsteds at Winchester, said that my Lord of Norfolk and my Lady were on pilgrimage at Our Lady (Walsingham) on foot. . . .[1]

Pilgrimage was a practice open to all sectors of society, to both sexes and to rich and poor. While it was not a religious act that was advocated as essential or compulsory for Christians in the way that it is for some religions today, it was nevertheless recommended by the Church as a means of commending one's soul to God, of receiving forgiveness for sin, as a method of purchasing indulgences (to release the subject from specific lengths of time in Purgatory) and, most commonly, in order to invoke the aid of specific saints in matters relating to health, wealth and family.

In her fourteenth-century handbook of manners for noblewomen, Christine de Pisan recommends that it is acceptable for noble ladies to undertake pilgrimages so long as they do so with a contrite heart: 'no lady is so important that it is shameful or unsuitable for her to go devoutly and humbly to pardons or to visit churches or holy places'.[2] Three centuries earlier, the eleventh-century chronicler Ralph Glaber, in his commentary on the increased popularity of pilgrimage to the Holy Land, had remarked specifically on the increased number of both rich and poor women visiting the Holy Sepulchre shrine:

> At this same time so innumerable a multitude began to flock from all parts of the world to the sepulchre of our Saviour at Jerusalem, as no man could before have expected; for the lower orders of people led the way, after whom came those of middle rank, and then all the greatest kings and counts and bishops; lastly (a thing which had never come to pass before), many noble ladies and poorer women journeyed thither. For many purposed and desired to die before they should see their homes again. . . .[3]

Some widowed noblewomen chose pilgrimage as the expression of their religious observance and followed the completion of their journey by joining a nunnery, or taking a vow of chastity. Aside from the conventional involvements of such women in charitable works and the giving of material support to the Church and the poor, pilgrimage was another route by which they could express their piety in pursuit of their personal salvation. The pilgrimage activity of those English women pilgrims of noble or royal birth can sometimes be traced through Privy Purse expenses which record the large sums they bestowed on shrines. For example, a list of expenses for 1502/3 shows that Elizabeth of York, the wife of Henry VII, left numerous donations to pilgrimage shrines including those of Our Lady of Walsingham and of Sudbury.

Naturally, the pilgrimage experience of those of noble or royal birth could be vastly different to that of the majority of people. Difficulties were smoothed over by the assistance and protection afforded by the luxury of large retinues, which might include yeomen and horses; their wealth assured them comfortable lodgings and adequate provisions en route. An example was the late wife of a twelfth-century knight, Lady of Wormgay (Wormegey), who requested to undertake a pilgrimage to Rome and Cologne with her impressive retinue of twelve men, twelve horses and all her worldly goods.[4] Noteworthy too is the record of the permission granted for the projected pilgrimage of Elizabeth Luttrell and her husband Sir Andrew to Santiago de Compostela in 1361, which ordered:

> without delay to have delivered to Andrew one ship out of the ships not arrested for the passage of our beloved and faithful Richard de Stafford . . . in either of the ports of Dartmouth or Plymouth where Andrew shall choose to embark. The ship should be suitable for the passage of Andrew and Elizabeth, and twenty-four persons, men and women, and twenty-four horses in their company.[5]

Maria, daughter of the Duke of Bourbon, was afforded similar comfort by virtue of her status when in July 1329 Pope John XXII granted that her father might accompany her on pilgrimage 'with a fitting escort in four armed galleys, and all those in the said galley may visit the Holy Sepulchre . . .'.[6]

Equally, a letter from Sir John Paston of 1471 indicates the excitement generated by the passage of a royal pilgrimage: 'The King Edward [Edward IV] and his Queen and many other people are riding and going to Canterbury, men say that never have so many people on a pilgrimage been seen all at once . . .'[7]

While the conspicuous nature of such a large pilgrimage entourage might well attract the unwanted attention of opportunist thieves, on occasion it might also offer safe conduct for those able to travel with their party. Certainly, safety in numbers was key to any pilgrimage journey, for men and women alike. Nonetheless, given the conspicuously lavish entourage of Margaret Florentyne, it is remarked by some of Margery's old companions with whom she reconvenes at Rome that such a woman had been able to arrive safely. For

Margery, a woman travelling alone with only Richard, a hunchback for company, her prospect of safe arrival was greater as one of Margaret's party.

In his study of *Miracles and Pilgrims* (1977), Ronald Finucane shows that smaller, local shrines were the most popular pilgrimage destinations for women of the lower orders, while the rich and powerful, on the other hand, had the resources to travel further and so might choose to visit any of the fashionable overseas pilgrimage venues. However, even those of higher status and greater wealth were required to seek licence and safe-conduct for their journeys abroad; for example, the Countess of Devon's request for protection for her pilgrimage to Pontigny is noted in the Calendars of Patent Rolls for 1254. Doubtless, it was the elevated rank and powerful position of Queen Elizabeth of Hungary, mother of Lajos I (Louis the Great) of Poland, that helped facilitate her journey not only to Rome in 1343–4 but to Aachen, where she founded a Hungarian chapel within the cathedral, and to Marburg and Cologne in 1357 in the company of the emperor Charles IV.

Most commonly, it is male members of the nobility – kings, their male retainers and knights – who are found on pilgrimage while their wives or queens accompany them. However, there do exist examples of women undertaking such journeys in the company of other women, their female neighbours and matrons. While pilgrimage held many gender-specific dangers for women, those of high birth might be considered yet more vulnerable if they travelled without their husbands or at least a large retinue for protection. Alternatively, such women might choose to send proxy pilgrims in their place, as those of the lower classes were able to do if they were frail or ill. This was the case for Queen Isabella of Bavaria (d. 1435) who, plagued by constant concerns for her faltering health and excessive weight, chose to do just that. Her status is reflected in the demands she makes of her proxy pilgrims. She is in a position to choose the saints she wishes to petition regardless of location and, not surprisingly, they are those associated with health. She sends three chaplains to different holy sites including a shrine of St Lazarus, as well as another proxy to the shrine of Our Lady of Blanc Mesnil. She equips the latter with a 15lb candle instructing him to burn 1lb of the wax at the shrine each day, for fifteen days.

It is important to note here that on account of their land and wealth, noble and gentrywomen would have been expected to be generous benefactresses, making grants to religious houses and religious endowments as well as undertaking pilgrimage. Noble families might also form a connection with a particular religious house or foundation, making grants there and requesting special masses, a connection that would be maintained down the generations. For example, the will of Anne, Countess Stafford, dated 1438, details the connections that were maintained with various religious foundations through her own family line.[8]

Religious education would also play an important part in a noblewoman's upbringing and along with the growth of literacy among their class throughout the fifteenth century came more widespread personal use of Books of Hours and other devotional material. Good works or acts of charity were regarded as integral to such women's role in society; their household accounts often show regular almsgiving, observance of the traditional Maundy Thursday aid to the poor, as well as the donations to almshouses and hospitals that were made in wills. In her fourteenth-century handbook for women, Christine de Pisan notes that '[the] noble lady will not think it beneath her to visit women in childbed, both rich and poor. She will give to the poor for the love of God . . . she will conduct herself so charitably in every way and show herself to be kind and humane towards her subjects. . . .'[9]

Geoffrey de la Tour-Landry, also writing in the fourteenth century reiterates these values in his own counsel to his three daughters:

The pleasure of all good women ought to be to visit and feed the poor and fatherless children and to nourish and clothe young little children, as did a holy woman who was countess of Mans, who always fed thirty fatherless children and said it was her recreation. Therefore she was loved by God and had a good life and death.[10]

Not only were such pilgrims expected to be generous benefactors to holy shrines, but it seems there was a kind of arrangement operating on the part of the Church for those vows of pilgrimage by the rich that could not be fulfilled. Having vowed to undertake a pilgrimage to Santiago on behalf of his mother Queen Margaret, her son Edmund of Woodstock found that he required dispensation from his vow for political reasons. This was granted on condition that he donate to the cathedral in Santiago a sum commensurate with the cost of his pilgrimage had he undertaken it, a journey that would, of course, have involved much greater expense than would have been available to the average pilgrim.

In another instance, Joan de Bar le Duc, Countess of Warenne and Surrey, already away on her pilgrimage and bound for Santiago de Compostela, had to request dispensation in 1355 to return to England, cutting short her pilgrimage on account of her husband's death. She is granted a year and a half to allow her to return home and settle her husband's affairs before her vow was reactivated. She had actually requested three years.[11]

Royal pilgrims might also find themselves the recipients of special dispensation where the receipt of indulgences was concerned. These were governed by the Church and certified forgiveness for past sins, saving the recipient from a fixed duration in Purgatory. Chiefly authorised by the Pope, shrines assumed quantitative value relative to the amount of remission time they offered, so that, for example, indulgences of up to seven years were available to pilgrims to St Peter's in Rome on major feast days. For the duration of 1300, Rome's first Jubilee year, Pope Boniface VIII had offered plenary indulgence to all those visiting the basilicas of Sts Peter and Paul in Rome. Originally announced as a centenary celebration, Boniface's successor Pope Clement VI yielded to increased demands that the Jubilee's observance be increased to every fifty years.

By 1350, pilgrims were required to visit the Basilica of St John in the Lateran, as well as those of Ss Peter and Paul if they wished to receive full forgiveness of sins. It seems that many royal personages began to look for ways of circumventing the wearying and time-consuming task of undertaking a pilgrimage to Rome, although, naturally, they still wanted to benefit from the Jubilee indulgences. Edward III sent his preacher as his proxy, though Edward would still be the ultimate beneficiary of the indulgence, while Philip VI of Spain cited old age and frailty as reasons for staying at home. Initially, the Pope, had stated that no one would be granted the Jubilee indulgence unless they visited the designated shrines in person, regardless of rank or physical condition. However, his attitude must have been tempered with time as the following year Edward III was granted his Jubilee indulgence in exchange for a sum equal to the cost of his journey to Rome. Others such as Queen Elizabeth of Hungary were allowed to appoint a confessor to undertake their pilgrimage in their place and still be granted the full indulgence.

This trend appears to have continued when a Jubilee was announced for 1390, bringing it forward a decade. Simultaneously, the Basilica of Santa Maria Maggiore was added to the list of churches that had to be visited by pilgrims in Rome in order that they might benefit from the indulgence. The Queen of Denmark wrote to Pope Boniface IX requesting that she be granted the indulgence of both the 1390 Jubilee as well as of the following, unofficial Jubilee of 1400; and he duly conferred on her 'the same indulgence and remission as those who visit the basilicas of St Peter, St Paul, St John Lateran, and S. Maria Maggiore in this present year . . .'.[12]

Regardless of status, fear of death and Purgatory crossed every social divide, so that the necessity for receiving spiritual guidance, forgiveness of sins and the ever-popular indulgence was just as important to the rich and high born as it was for the poor and lowly. However, as we have seen, a position of power and the ability to gain the Pope's ear sometimes allowed the rich to benefit from such Jubilee indulgences without having to go through the same channels as the lower classes. However, some of the reasons offered for their release from such journeys are very similar, including old age and frailty. It is fair to assume also that the highest born such as royalty and the most powerful might have been kept away by the commitments of their office. From the perspective of the Church, the pecuniary offerings of the rich were always welcome and the granting of indulgence in such instances might have appeared a most acceptable alternative.

It is possible that in the early Middle Ages in particular there was a trend for pilgrimage among the nobility with certain shrines attracting a more distinguished clientèle. However, with the progress of time and the increased popularity of pilgrimage across the social spectrum, such distinctions became blurred. In its infancy, pilgrimage was seen to be very popular among the wealthy and noble. One of our earliest examples was Paula; a well-educated woman from an illustrious Roman family, who travelled to Bethlehem with her daughter. In a letter to her friend Marcella in Rome, trying to persuade her to join them in the holy places, she seems to point to the idea of pilgrimage for the high born: 'Whosoever is noblest in Gaul comes hither.'

In his study of medieval pilgrimage, Jonathan Sumption argues that the phenomenon of greater popularity of pilgrimage among the noble classes came to an end at the close of the twelfth century, when 'the established shrines of Europe began to lose their hold on educated minds'.[13] He blames a sense of apathy and the consequences of war for the apparent abandonment of such popular shrines by their nobler visitors. However, it is possible that the increasing popularity of such shrines with the inevitable overcrowding and too frequent scenes of pandemonium at the most popular, conspired to persuade some of the rich and powerful that it would be better to seek other means of achieving remission from sin, either through charitable acts or monetary donations. Certainly, there is, too, some evidence of class tensions in accounts that describe pilgrims of all backgrounds thrown together, for instance on pilgrim galleys. Many shrines that had once been considered destinations exclusive to the upper classes had come to enjoy wider recognition and hence increased visitor numbers. From the perspective of the more privileged, this may have made them less attractive or favourable as destinations. The later popularity of newer, less fashionable shrines among the nobility, such as that at Le Puy, would seem to endorse this idea and suggests that for some of the nobility at least, a sense of exclusivity at their chosen shrine was desirable.

The numbers of nobility on pilgrimage at holy shrines appeared to revive with a surge of pilgrimage activity in the fifteenth century. Some still attempted to receive the spiritual benefits of pilgrimage without having to make the journey and yet others set out on theirs with ostentatious pomp and show.

One shrine in England that appeared to retain its popularity with royalty was the holy house at Walsingham. Regardless of means or social status, women pilgrims tended to find themselves visiting shrines for very similar reasons, family matters being the most common. In the case of royalty, those familiar issues of fertility and conception could be all the more pressing with the requirement to produce a healthy male heir. Such concerns brought kings and their consorts, as well as queens, to shrines to petition for assistance, with Walsingham consistently favoured for such matters. Among those who travelled to Walsingham for such reasons were Richard II and his Queen, Henry II, Edward I, Edward II, David Bruce, King of Scotland (under a safe conduct from the English king), Henry VII and finally Henry VIII with his Queen, Catherine of Aragon. Indeed, in his early years, Henry was a great supporter of the shrine, staying at nearby Barsham Manor.

Independently of her husband, Catherine of Aragon also exhibited a marked devotion to the shrine of Our Lady of Walsingham and inscribed in her will of 1536 the request that someone be appointed to undertake pilgrimage there on her behalf after her death. In the early years of her marriage to Henry VIII, in March 1518, she had also visited the shrine of St Frideswide, Oxford.

Some female sovereigns on pilgrimage themselves established shrines that came to enjoy cult status and followings. Perhaps most famous of these women was the mother of Constantine the Great, Empress Helena, who in AD 326 purportedly uncovered the True Cross and then with her son, marked out several of the venerated sites of the Holy Land that subsequently came to be visited by pilgrims in their thousands.

In 1125 the daughter of Henry I of England, Empress Matilda, embarked on a similar undertaking. She went on pilgrimage to Santiago de Compostela where she reportedly recovered the hand of St James, Compostela's resident saint, which she brought back to England. The provision of this sacred vestige saw the establishment of Reading Abbey which her father Henry I had instructed to be built in 1121. The abbey was now in the enviable position of owning its own holy relic and one which, in addition, was credited with the performance of curative miracles, restoring the health of those suffering from a variety of ailments. The monks of Reading Abbey also benefited; the abbey's finances were generously increased through the offerings of the numerous pilgrims attracted by its relic. The abbey became the final resting place of Henry I, who was buried there at his own request.

In the struggles against the infidel in the Holy Land, on occasion royal women might also find themselves accompanying their husbands on pilgrimages in support of the Christian cause overseas. In 1270, Eleanor of Castile, wife of Edward I, accompanied her husband to the Holy Land on the Fifth Crusade.[14] At one point Edward was reportedly attacked by an assassin and stabbed with a poisoned dagger. He managed to kill his assailant and apocryphal tales tell of how Eleanor sucked the poison from the wound and saved his life.[15] This romantic embellishment of the original legend became popularly circulated.

Eleanor accompanied Edward I again, in his battle against Baibars, the leading Muslim sultan. Returning home to England in 1286 she bequeathed a host of gems and relics to several different

94

religious houses. Such acts by royal women, facilitated by their wealth and positions of power, could help to subsidise and endorse pilgrimage practice through the embellishment of shrines by providing the holy articles that came to be their most powerful draw.

In the twelfth century, Eleanor of Aquitaine accompanied her then husband, Louis VII of France, on the Second Crusade to Antioch. Her story is somewhat different and has engendered much debate and controversy among historians. William of Tyre, a contemporary historian of the Crusades, highlights the alleged misconduct of Eleanor on this expedition, claiming that she conducted an affair with her uncle, Raymond of Antioch. William states that Raymond seduced Eleanor in order to exact vengeance on her husband for their political differences and that 'contrary to [Eleanor's] royal dignity, she disregarded her marriage vows and was unfaithful to her husband'. It seems that she also made indiscreet attempts to stay behind with her uncle after Louis had decided to depart, although Raymond was then killed in battle in 1149. Eleanor continued to attract controversy and gossip after her divorce from Louis VII and subsequent marriage to Henry II of England. The stigma of her alleged misconduct while on crusade continued to colour the comments of chroniclers and gossips well beyond her lifetime.

However, Eleanor's infidelity to her first husband's bed while on the crusade has never been substantiated, and some argue that she was guilty of nothing more than siding with Raymond against her husband in political matters. What is significant here, however, is Eleanor's involvement in the political dimension of their sojourn in the Holy Land. That Eleanor should play an active political role went against the norm of contemporary female behaviour, even of those married to kings. In fact, she became known for her political involvement. It is partly her atypical personality that laid her more open to intrigue, in this particular instance, a situation further fuelled perhaps by her marriage to Henry II less than two months after her divorce from Louis.

Of course, just like their humbler counterparts, the most usual reasons for women of the nobility to find themselves on pilgrimage related to their roles as mothers, wives and widows. Records show that Elizabeth of York (1465–1503), wife of Henry VII and daughter of Edward IV, went on a pilgrimage to Walsingham after the deaths of two children, an infant son and her four-year-old daughter Elizabeth. The Walsingham shrine was dedicated to the Virgin Mary and thus had a strong resonance for medieval women petitioners seeking her mothering and nurturing intercession. Elizabeth also made donations to several other shrines through proxy pilgrims, namely a priest, Sir William Barton and one Richard Mylner of Bynfield. The majority of the shrines to which Elizabeth of York chose to bequeath funds were associated with the Virgin, including those of Our Lady at Walsingham, Sudbury, Woolpit, Ipswich and Berking, near the Tower of London.[16]

Interestingly, Elizabeth's royal status did not affect her choice of pilgrimage shrine, nor did her methods of devotion as a queen set her apart from women of the lower orders. Her wealth may have enabled her to make more generous donations to the shrines she chose or, indeed, have allowed her to muster more proxy pilgrims on her behalf to a larger array of holy sites, but her motivations as a woman and a mother were the same, so rendering her privileged status immaterial with regard to pilgrimage.

The Virgin was a particularly potent symbol to women pilgrims because of her associations with childbearing and fertility, making such shrines an obvious choice on which Elizabeth might focus her petitioning devotions. The fact that many of her donations were made in August 1502, when it appears she was pregnant, could also indicate a pregnancy-related illness or anxiety.

In December 1502, two months before she was due to deliver her child, Elizabeth did something else that was a familiar and common practice among medieval women. She paid a monk for a 'Lady gyrdelle' of the type worn by women to facilitate their labour and the delivery of a healthy newborn. That Elizabeth would have been able to request the loan of one of the venerated girdles displayed as relics in monasteries and abbeys across the country is indicative of her status, but her hopes, expectations and fears as a mother-to-be and the methods of divine intercession to which she resorted were no different from those employed by women of every walk of life.

Elizabeth had a girl, Katherine, who was born and died on 2 February 1503. Elizabeth died of a post-pregnancy infection nine days later, on her thirty-seventh birthday. She was also mother of the future Henry VIII, who would come to play a significant role in the practice of pilgrimage, as we shall see. Despite her status as a princess and then wife of Henry VII, throughout her difficult pregnancy and the deaths of two of her children, Elizabeth of York seems to have demonstrated the widespread female devotion to the Virgin as the Holy Mother. She also had strong associations with the shrines of Our Lady, Marian imagery and symbolism in general and believed in the efficacy of holy relics and talismans as means of divine intercession. Such behaviour would seem to indicate that choice of pilgrimage destination had more to do with the type of help required than with the status of the individual pilgrim.

Like many other women of her day, Elizabeth of York felt a strong affinity with another female saint, St Birgitta (Bridget) of Sweden. In this instance, she was able to use her position to commission the printing of St Bridget's prayers by William Caxton in 1490. As in the case of many women in the event of their death, a proxy pilgrim was assigned to undertake a pilgrimage in Elizabeth's name in order to pray for the safe delivery of her soul, in this case at the shrine of Our Lady at Willesden in London.

Elizabeth de Burgh was another enthusiastic pilgrim and donor to holy shrines. Born in 1295 to Princess Joan, daughter of Edward I, and Gilbert, 9th Earl de Clare, she was a thrice-married, wealthy heiress with an impressive pilgrimage record. Her pilgrimage journeys included those to Walsingham, Canterbury and the Holy Rood at Bromholm. A papal letter also indicates another planned pilgrimage to the Holy Land and Santiago de Compostela, of which she requested the vow be transmuted into other charitable acts on account of her advancing years, albeit she was only forty-eight. The offering that she would have made to the shrine of St James was sent on to Compostela.

However, it was Elizabeth de Burgh's connection with the shrine at Walsingham that was strongest. It was under her in 1347 that a Franciscan priory was built on the edge of the village, much to the Augustinian Canon of Walsingham's chagrin. He was concerned that it would divert the pilgrims' custom away from the Holy House. Yet there is no doubt that Elizabeth de Burgh was a very generous donor. In her will she also left the sum of 100 marks to enable three men-at-arms to undertake a pilgrimage to the Holy Land to pray for the deliverance of her soul.[17]

It was relatively common practice for women of royal and noble rank to request in their wills that pilgrimage be undertaken on their behalf. Naturally, as with such journeys embarked upon during their lifetimes, these pilgrimages, financed by the wealth of the testators, could be elaborate and far-reaching. Such was the case for the opulent Scandinavian Queen, Margaret of Denmark, who in September 1410 requested that pilgrimages be made in her honour to comprise the length and breadth of Christendom, beginning with shrines in her own Scandinavian dominion and ranging as far afield as Santiago de Compostela and Sinai.

Every level of medieval society was permeated by the belief that the more or holier the shrines at which prayers were said and supplications made, or the more saints' holy places at which one's name was invoked, the greater the likelihood of salvation or deliverance from a particular malady or danger. Naturally, and thanks largely to the greater resources, it was a religious practice of which the privileged could take best advantage. The equally widespread belief in Purgatory and the need to receive absolution for one's sins meant that many of the most generous and notable shrine offerings and pilgrimages were the result of provisions made in wills to be carried out after the testator's death.

EIGHT

Female Saints and their Shrines

For Trusteth it wel, it is an impossible
That any clerk wol speke good of wives,
But if it be of hooly seintes lives . . .[1]

There was a plethora of female saints who were widely acclaimed and adored by those who visited their shrines as petitioners and devotees. Many were identified with particular causes and had specific associations in the minds of their followers, perceived as intermediaries for the familial and domestic matters popularly presented at shrines by women suppliants. Credited with the greatest influence the Virgin Mary was invoked by mothers for help with matters relating to conception and childbirth. Women martyrs, saints and figureheads thus played a significant role as the maternal, receptive and compassionate figures of the divine liturgy with nurturing qualities that mirrored those of ordinary medieval woman and thus commanded a large popular following among them.

The housekeeper saint, Zita (1218–72), was invoked by medieval women for help with practical and domestic matters; they might ask her help, for instance, to recover lost keys. Zita had been a servant for a family in Lucca in Italy at the age of twelve. It was said that she repeatedly got into trouble for helping the poor by donating her own food and that of her master. Consequently, she is often depicted carrying loaves as well as keys and is today still considered a patron of domestics, servants, butlers, housemaids and so on – and continues to be invoked for the recovery of lost keys.

St Zita had made pilgrimage to the shrines of St Mary Magdalene, St Peter and also San Jacopo di Piodio in the neighbourhood of Pisa, built during her lifetime by the female mystic, Bona of Pisa. Bona had established the shrine to serve as a local outpost for those unable to make the journey to Santiago de Compostela, among whom may well have been Zita in her role as a housekeeper. In the sixteenth century, in his scathing attacks on the practice of pilgrimage and the 'misplaced' worship of saints and relics, Sir Thomas More satirised the role of St Zita, saying that housewives spent more time going on pilgrimage to invoke her help in the finding of lost keys than the keys were worth in the first place.

In addition to shrines visited for their association with female concerns there were also a host of sites venerated on account of their endorsement by women pilgrims who claimed to have received divine intercession or cures there. The type of miracles on offer and the mythology of the saint were highly significant. Most often, these were the shrines of female saints with whom wives, widows, mothers and mothers-to-be could most easily associate, as well as of saints linked to cures for specifically female ailments. It is hardly surprising that medieval women, whose lives were centred on domestic life and child-rearing, would gravitate towards those female-oriented shrines where their supplications were most likely to bring help with the affairs of family, hearth and home. In the context of the reality of their everyday lives, it is easy enough to appreciate the profound impact of the Virgin Mary and Marian imagery in the Middle Ages for medieval women in particular.

It did not always follow that these saints were female, however. Another shrine that enjoyed a popular female following was that of a Norfolk man, Godric of Finchale; it was located near Durham and drew large numbers of local women pilgrims and those of the lower orders. Women were excluded from approaching the shrine of St Cuthbert at the nearby cathedral priory of Durham and it seems that this led to the increased popularity of its neighbouring shrine of Godric. In at least one instance a female pilgrim claims to have been redirected by St Cuthbert to Finchale for her cure. The earthly remains of Godric began to be credited with performing miracles in June 1172 and we learn that of 244 miracles recorded, two-thirds of the subjects were women.[2]

Although never formally canonised, Godric (1065–1170) was a popular medieval saint who had spent the last sixty years of his life as a hermit in Norfolk. His devotion to Christianity had begun with a meeting with St Cuthbert in Lindisfarne after which, having made pilgrimages to Jerusalem, he settled in Finchale as a hermit for his final years. In that time his reputation grew to the extent that such notable figures as Thomas Becket and Pope Alexander III sought him out for his wisdom and counsel.

Godric exhibited qualities of nurturing and tenderness and a particular fondness for animals. Stories recall his protection of the animals that lived near his forest home: he is reported to have hidden a stag from hunters and to have invited snakes to warm themselves at his fire. He is sometimes depicted dressed in white as a hermit with a stag. Godric was also a lover of poetry and the song 'Sainte nicholaes' by him is believed to be the earliest surviving example of English lyric verse. It was said that such songs, lyrics and music were divinely imparted to him during his visions.

While medieval women probably found themselves able to associate with Godric's nurturing tendencies, it is likely that they also recognised him as an intercessory with the Virgin, whom he reported appearing to him in several visions. His biographer Reginald recorded four songs that Godric said had been taught to him in visions by the Blessed Virgin, his dead sisters and others. Godric also built a wattle oratory and later a small stone church dedicated to St Mary:

> At his first coming he had built an oratory, and one day saw above the altar two young and very lovely maids: the one of them, Mary Magdalene, the other the Mother of God: and the Mother of God put her hand upon his head and taught him to sing after her this prayer: *Mary Holy Virgin, mother of Jesus Christ of Nazareth, Hold, shield and help thy Godric, Take him, bring him soon to the Kingdom of God with thee.*[3]

Not only could male saints attract large female followings, but those shrines initially popular predominantly with women might also come to be the focus of male pilgrims and visitors over time. Such was the case of the shrine of Frideswide of Oxford. As with the shrine of Godric of Finchale, Frideswide's popularity was largely local with most pilgrims travelling to the shrine from within a 40-mile radius. Less is known about the earlier life of Frideswide than of Godric except that she was of local, Saxon, origin and that a collection of posthumous miracles attributed to her were collated in the twelfth century. After her father's death, so the story goes, a local king tried to force himself on her in marriage, to which she responded by escaping in a boat and living her remaining years in exile. It was during this time that Frideswide established a reputation for herself as a healer and ascetic. A small village on the edge of Oxford called Binsey is host to a church and a well to whose water is attributed the curative powers of St Frideswide.

It might be that Frideswide's popularity with women suppliants was two-fold, due in part to her interest as a woman of local, historical significance as well as to the fact that she embodied the almost formulaic characteristics of other female saints as a maiden living an anchoritic life of self-denial, asceticism, prayer, visions and displaying a propensity for healing. However, it was not long before her shrine began to attract male petitioners, something which Finucane explains thus: 'it may be that women . . . led the way and that men turned to Godric after several cures had demonstrated to them that the cult was no mere flight of female fancy'.[4]

It was Frideswide's burial in her Oxford nunnery in the eighth century and the subsequent building of a church there in the twelfth that saw the beginnings of her popularity as a saint with healing powers. The translation of Frideswide's bones to a new shrine in 1180 attracted many pilgrims and anticipation of miracles followed, placing St Frideswide's on the map at a time when the cult of Thomas Becket also enjoyed great popularity. As with Godric, roughly two-thirds of the 108 miracles attributed to Frideswide concerned women beneficiaries. Frideswide was never officially canonised, although her reputation spread well beyond her locality, reaching Canterbury's cathedral priory where she received honorary recognition. The story of Frideswide's rise to popularity is also a notable example of the important role that women could play in creating and extending the appeal of certain shrines through retailing their reported miracle activity by word of mouth, thus attracting many more women visitors, and in this case also arousing the interest of some male petitioners. In this instance, this was sufficient to support the popularity of the shrine (along with its endorsement by Canterbury) without Frideswide ever having been officially canonised and without the international fame and lavish setting of, say, the shrine of St Thomas Becket.

From the end of the twelfth century, like Godric's at Finchale, Becket's shrine was another example of a venerated site connected with a male figure that nevertheless attracted a wide, popular female following. This may be partly due to the gift attributed to him of assisting women in childbirth and pregnancy. Certainly, of those miracles recorded at the shrine by the monks William and Benedict, many concerned conception, pregnancy and birth. (We must not forget that childbirth was a high-risk experience for medieval women with significantly high mortality rates for both mother and child.)

Women might also employ holy relics associated with conception and childbirth in order to aid the safe delivery of mother and child. As an example, Margery Kempe meets a woman who has a miniature figure of Christ that she 'sett . . . in worshipful wyfys lappys', a gesture that is a symbolic blessing of the womb.

Women might also ask the help of the Virgin and saints during childbearing in a subconscious acknowledgement of the common recognition of the sins of Eve as the source of the pains of labour, afflicting women ever after as the punishment for Eve's alliance with the serpent. A fourteenth-century book of lessons for the daughters of a noble knight recounted that had Eve not sinned in this way, then women 'shold haue had children without any dolour or peyne . . .'.[5]

Aside from the efficacy of prayer and potential miracles associated with shrines, they might also provide more tangible aid. Pilgrims believed certain objects and souvenirs purchased from shrines were invested with supernatural healing qualities and acted as protective talismans and lucky charms. They took away ampoules of holy water as well as handfuls of dust or earth from the environs of the holy shrine, believing both to be infused with the powers of the saint. Of course, gazing upon the original relics was the ultimate goal, particularly if the pilgrims received the cure or assistance for which they hoped. In one instance a widow and mother on pilgrimage sent back a pilgrim badge from Walsingham in a letter to one of her four sons as a personal assurance that it would secure the safety and health of her children in her absence by virtue of it being sent from Walsingham. Additionally, those items and souvenirs that were taken away from shrines by pilgrims could be used within the home as a kind of secondary, perambulatory relic.

An integral part of the pilgrimage tradition was the expectation that at their destination there was a beautifully adorned reliquary containing the holy relics which the pilgrims had come to behold. Such relics were the intermediary force or conduit between the spiritual and corporeal worlds. That pilgrims also expected it to be an object of visual wonder seems to have been widely accepted, so that great efforts went into the embellishment and presentation of the holy relics, a process that has fairly been described by some scholars as employment of the modern concept of 'attractive packaging'. Then, as now, the purpose was to draw the attention of pilgrims to what its clerical and lay supporters hoped might become a much talked about shrine with its splendid reliquary, secondly that the relics, bedecked in precious jewels and gems, might take on an even greater ethereal charm and otherworldly quality. After all, the pilgrims did not always get to see the actual relics, more often being greeted by a dramatically adorned shrine or reliquary casket. The tomb of Thomas Becket at Canterbury was just such a shrine, adorned with a splendid array of sapphires, gold, rubies and gems, all at great expense, enough, we are told, to fill twenty-six carts when Henry VIII dissolved the cathedral priory at Canterbury and had its riches carried away.[6]

That pilgrims had come to expect this kind of showy and costly presentation of holy relics is also implied by the reported disappointment of one female pilgrim who arrived at a shrine to find that no such efforts or expense had been lavished on it: 'seeing that the saint's tomb did not glitter with gold and silver, she uttered a contemptuous guffaw. . . . Then, rushing back home, she bade her friends retrace their steps saying "you won't find anything holy in that place".'[7] Interesting here is the clear association made between the power of the saint and the embellishment of his shrine and that his lacking 'holiness' is a measure of the absence of costly adornment.

Of significance too is the absence of any gifts from previous pilgrims as there is nothing to advertise the power of the saint's intercessory ability. Such *ex-voto* offerings left by pilgrims in recognition of their cure at the shrine would have acted as important evidence for subsequent pilgrims and served to reaffirm the shrine's power, as well as bolstering the latters' faith in receiving a cure themselves. Such offerings sometimes consisted of wax models representing the afflicted part of the body now cured. The church of Our Lady at Rocamadour was said to display so many of these that pilgrims even began to doubt their authenticity, their sheer numbers arousing suspicions as to whether the monks were in fact making them themselves.

Naturally, in the eyes of the Church and the staff of religious buildings associated with venerated saints, holy relics could became the main draw for pilgrims and their custom, particularly if they had been shown to work miracles. Helena, the mother of Constantine the Great, was one of the earliest known participants in the trade in relics, and several holy items were brought back to England from the Holy Land by Crusaders where she had purportedly discovered the True Cross and the Holy Sepulchre in AD 326. The fall of Constantinople in 1204 saw another influx of bones from the churches of the East. Relics included any article associated with the life or death of a saint or venerated figure. For the holy family, these included the Virgin's tunic, her breast milk or her hair, as well as more abstract articles including the captured breath or blood of Christ in a glass phial, all venerated objects of wonder. Abbot Guibert of Nogent even related how he saw a relic-monger holding up a box which he claimed contained a piece of the very bread chewed by Our Lord at the Last Supper.

Most highly prized and venerated were those articles concerned with Christ's crucifixion so that the demand for pieces of the True Cross was overwhelming and although some of the cross was said to have made its way straight to Rome, more churches came to claim ownership of its fragments than was physically possible. By 1561, it was disparagingly noted by Calvin that the portions of the True Cross in churches across Europe were enough to load a large ship![8]

In their enthusiasm for holy relics as the physical means whereby assistance from the spiritual world could be channelled, devotees might become the unwitting victims in the trade of fake or even stolen relics. King Canute's queen Emma was thought to have bought several relics whose authenticity could not be proven, including the arm of St Bartholomew purchased from the Bishop of Benevento in 1017.[9] By the fourteenth and fifteenth centuries, the problem of fake relics had become so widespread that it prompted Calvin to comment that one could no longer be sure on what it was that he/she was bestowing their affections, so that the buyer was at risk of venerating the bones of a dog, horse, or thief, or even an article attributed to the Virgin that had actually belonged to a prostitute. Chaucer's Pardoner famously deceives his patrons by showing them 'pigges bones' that he professes to be the genuine article, along with a pillowcase which he cunningly displays as the Virgin's veil.

Other such relics included girdles, blessed at the elected shrine or brought into close enough contact with its relics that it might absorb some of their supernatural healing power. These girdles were particularly cherished by women during labour and childbirth. By the early twelfth century, St Anselm's girdle was being loaned out by Canterbury Cathedral as a relic to lay around pregnant women's abdomens to facilitate an easier birth. Queens were allowed access to the most prized girdle, that which was believed to have belonged to the Virgin Mary. It was despatched from Westminster to Gascony to assist Henry III's wife, Eleanor of Provence. Those without access to a girdle might lay a parchment over their belly perhaps bearing a cross or else a mark resembling the wound in Christ's side, along with a written promise of a successful delivery. If it was considered likely that the mother would die before the baby could be safely delivered, the Church permitted the midwife to open the womb so effectively performing a Caesarean section.

Of course, pride of place among the saints venerated by ordinary medieval women was accorded to the Virgin Mary and her cult as ultimate figurehead and potent symbol for their own roles as childbearers and mothers. There were several shrines dedicated to the Virgin across Europe and these came to be termed shrines of Our Lady.

Aside from her association with family matters, the Virgin was also associated with other miraculous if more mundane interventions. Abbot Guibert of Nogent reports how in a procession of relics of the Virgin through the city of Angers, a woman who had been married as a young girl approached. She had been wearing a wedding band since girlhood and, as she had gained weight along with her years, her hands had eventually swollen to encompass the ring in the flesh of her finger so that it could not be removed:

> as she held out her hand to place the money she had brought, on the relics, the ring cracked and slipped from her hand amongst them. Beyond all description were the offerings of money by the people and of rings and necklaces by the women after they had seen and especially the women, how the Virgin Mother had shewn such favour to that woman in what she dared not ask herself.[10]

Guibert continues his description to note the celebratory awe of the event and, most interesting, that 'the canton of Tours had much joy at this showering of the sweet odours of our Lady's merits, who is common to all, but the people of Angers always boasted that in a special sense did the Mother of God belong to them'.[11]

Of course, the Virgin existed as one person in her lifetime and in death presided at her shrines as a spiritual force that could be invoked for special favour and intervention. The medieval world firmly believed that once deceased, the souls of such venerated figures could exist in several places at once or at least were transient, hence presiding over several shrines across Europe. The building of the Holy House at Walsingham is a good example of this, for it was believed that the Virgin had specially chosen this remote corner of Norfolk as her new resting place after Nazareth. We gain an inkling of the almost jealous attachment some communities might exhibit for their honoured saint, Angers claiming the Virgin as its own on account of the miracles she performed for them that day. Certainly, there also existed competition between different reliquary shrines in terms of the number of relics held and the level of miraculous activity the relics were capable of performing. The fact that the girl's predicament was apparently recognised by the Virgin and remedied without the need for supplication is of meritorius note, for Angers was a centre for miracle activity.

However, a study by Sumption shows that the earliest miracles attributed to the Virgin were not associated with any particular shrine (instead they were said to have been enacted far and wide across Germany, Spain and Italy), or even related to tangible relics. Nor is it until the tenth century that pilgrimage journeys to shrines associated with the Virgin were reportedly undertaken.[12] The introduction of the first holy relic of the Virgin, some of her hair found in a cathedral in Coutances by its bishop, was received with some scepticism on the grounds that there were no other relics of the Virgin known to exist. However, the cult of the Virgin seemed to spread exponentially after this and a host of relics said to be associated with her sprang into existence.

To the modern mind, the form that these relics took might well defy credibility in terms of what could conceivably have survived. Particularly problematic in this light are articles said to be preserved from the life of the Virgin. While items of the Crucifixion such as fragments of the True Cross might plausibly have been salvaged or kept for posterity by early Christians, there was nothing equivalent pertaining to Christ's mother. However, the medieval mind was perfectly receptive to the authenticity of all such relics including those as abstract as Christ's breath contained in a jar. For the Virgin, fragments of her hair, her tunic and samples of her breast milk came to be the most widely recognised and venerated vestiges of her life by pilgrims and religious houses alike. Indeed, the church of Santa Maria Maggiore in Rome even boasted possession of the original crib.

As with all relics, though, no individual relic was so sacred as to be safe from claims of ownership by other religious centres, so that, for example, Chartres, Verdun and other churches across France and Germany all claimed possession of the Virgin's tunic. In a similar vitriolic response to Calvin's, occasioned by the purported existence of several thousand fragments of the True Cross, and in line with contemporary criticism of a market flooded with supposedly genuine relics, Erasmus comments on the inordinate amount of reliquaries said to contain the Virgin's milk: 'she left us so much of her milk that it's scarcely credible a woman with only one child could have so much, even if the child had drunk none of it!' However, the nature of worship of the Virgin underwent dramatic transformation in the eleventh and twelfth centuries so that it became a widely popular cult for which pilgrims had come to accept 'a plurality of Virgins inhabiting defined places'.[13] At Coutances, the contemporary significance of the Virgin's influence was encapsulated by the prior of Sauxillanges during an outbreak of ergotism, caused by the ingestion of the fungus ergot found on infected cereal crops in 1206: 'She is the sovereign remedy for the sick . . . for she can obtain from her son all that she desires. She is merciful on our sins and relieves us in all our troubles.'[14] Considered second only to Christ, the Virgin was deemed a powerful and receptive intermediary. Hence such sites as Walsingham and the so-called 'Milk Grotto' in Bethlehem were held to be destinations of particular significance to women.

Men might also be drawn to visit such shrines. Henry VIII had been attracted by the familial associations of the shrine at Walsingham many times, partly as a result of his first wife, Catherine of Aragon's particular fealty to the shrine, but also to pray in his own right for a male heir and later to give thanks for the safe delivery of his new-born son by Jane Seymour. It is no coincidence that the small churches on the route to Walsingham such as at Houghton St Giles were also embellished with imagery of the female saints and the Virgin. Shrines with relics related to motherhood and childbearing were of course of peculiar significance to the female pilgrim, such as the relic of the Virgin's veil or tunic at Chartres,

An altarpiece by Francesco Botticini of St Jerome (left) with St Paula (centre) and St Eustochium, *c.* 1490. *(National Gallery, London)*

An illuminated letter of St Helena, the mother of Constantine the Great, Judas Cyriacus and a female attendant, finding the true cross. Italy, fifteenth century. (© *The British Library*)

Far left: St Bridget presents a message from Christ to a bishop, 'Revelations (Liber Celestis)', *c.* 1415. Cotton Claudius B.I, f.117. (© *The British Library*)

Left: A fourteenth-century marginal illumination of a woman beating her husband with a distaff, from the Lutrell Psalter. (© *British Library/ Bridgeman Art Library*)

Two first-century Gallo-Roman pilgrim votive statues from St Germain sur Seine, France. *(akg-images/Erich Lessing)*

Below, left: A misericord showing a woman depicted as a mermaid, St Laurence's Church, Ludlow, Shropshire. *(Author's Collection)*

Below, right: A misericord of a woman wearing a bridle to stop her gossiping in church, St Laurence's Church, Ludlow, Shropshire. *(Author's Collection)*

A carved thirteenth-century altarpiece at a church in Vadstena, Sweden. (© *Patrick Ward/CORBIS*)

A marginal illustration of a nun dancing with a friar, who is playing the bellows with a distaff, from an early fourteenth-century Book of Hours from Liège. Stowe 17 f.38. *(© The British Library)*

'The Joys of Marriage' – a woman with her husband while her lover is sneaking through the window. *(akg-images/Erich Lessing)*

A late fifteenth-century roundel showing pilgrims arriving at a hostel. *(© Photo RMN/Gérard Blot)*

A fourteenth-century illumination of St Godric at prayer. Ms Coton Faust. B.VI. f.16v. *(akg-images/British Library)*

Christine de Pisan at her writing desk, *c.* 1410–15. *(© British Library/ Bridgeman Art Library)*

The right wing of the triptych of St Eloi showing pilgrims praying at his shrine, Paris, *c.* 1530. *(akg-images/Amelot)*

A modern-day woman pilgrim on the Camino to Santiago de Compostela. *(Author's Collection)*

believed to ease labour pains. Elizabeth of York, wife of Henry VII, had lost two small children and was pregnant again in 1502 when she made several donations to shrines of Our Lady across the country. In December 1502, two months before she died in childbirth she had also paid a monk a sum for a 'Lady Gyrdelle' to help ensure an easier labour.

The relics on display at Walsingham and similar sites did not sit comfortably with every visitor, however. In his famous colloquy, Erasmus discussed the shrine of Walsingham with dry irony and has the character Ogygius quote from a letter of Mary, Mother of Jesus, in which she complains of the requests she receives from women visitors to the shrine: 'The maid cries, "Mary, give me a handsome and rich husband!" The wife cries, "Give me fine children!" The lady with child cries, "Grant me a happy time!" The old woman cries, "Grant I may live long without cough and thirst!" . . .'[15] At the very least, this extract emphasises the importance placed by women on the power of the Virgin as intercessor in such gender-specific issues as motherhood, childbearing and finding a good husband.

Many other female saints and figureheads were invoked by women in matters of fertility, childbearing, to promote the ability to suckle their newborn and to give protection to their offspring. On the road to Bethlehem, Rachel's Tomb was and still is frequented by women hoping to conceive. They engage in a ritual that involves tying red string seven times around the tomb, the string then being removed and worn by the supplicant. The visiting of holy sites thought to be imbued with the power to facilitate conception by women was a familiar practice. As early as AD 333, we have an account whose author is known only as the Pilgrim of Bordeaux. His visit to the Holy Land notes a Mount Syna and next to it a spring of which tradition held that all women who bathed in its waters would become pregnant.

There was a strong belief in the curative power of immersion in the water of holy springs or baths (such as those that existed at

Walsingham) and pilgrims undertook this practice where available as a kind of ritual cleansing. It was a re-enactment of the Baptism that absolved their sins and with it the ailments that were interpreted as a physical manifestation of sin. Equally, women pilgrims would seek out such springs or baths for the purpose of aiding their fertility and conception. Elsewhere in his account, the Pilgrim of Bordeaux describes a spring at Jericho associated with the prophet Elisha. However, this spring was earlier believed to have been cursed, so that any woman who drank from it found herself barren. Fortunately, Elisha was able to reverse the effects of the curse by ritually cleansing the spring in the Lord's name and by scattering salt there, 'Now if a woman drinks from it she will have children.'[16]

Women pilgrims would take the opportunity to drink or bathe in the waters of holy wells and to collect lead ampoules of holy water, such as could be purchased and taken away from the shrines of Becket in Canterbury or Walsingham in Norfolk. Also en route, pilgrims would be presented with many visual reminders of the saints whom they were journeying to invoke or, particularly, as on the way to Walsingham, of those Virgin martyrs who were portrayed on rood screens and elsewhere within churches. These included Ss Margaret and Dorothy, who were directly associated with the familial concerns that would have brought many women to the Walsingham shrine in the first place, Margaret as the patron saint of childbirth and Dorothy as the object of invocations against miscarriage.

Martyred female saints held a particular draw and potency for women pilgrims in the way that the martyred Thomas Becket had gripped the country in the twelfth century. To die a martyr's death in the name and faith of God was to die nobly and, to the medieval mind, meant a more direct route to heavenly paradise. One of the earliest and most powerfully depicted of these martyrs was St Catherine of Alexandria, frequently portrayed along with the implement of an early attempt at her martyrdom, the spike-studded wheel on which she was to be tied and broken. Legend has it that when she touched the wheel, it shattered into pieces before her. Catherine was therefore beheaded instead in AD 305, her body purportedly whisked away by angels at the moment of death. She was miraculously transported to Mount Sinai in Arabia, where two centuries later, in 527, Greek monks built the monastery of St Catherine which operates to this day. Both the accounts of Brother Felix Fabri of his trip to the Holy Land in 1483 and that of the errant knight Sir John Mandeville describe the shrine of St Catherine on Sinai. In his own inimitable style and most likely embellished with the tales and hearsay of other pilgrims, Mandeville described the display of the relics of St Catherine:

> After, they show you the head of St Catherine, and the cloth that it was wrapped in when the angels brought the body up to Sinai. And there, with that cloth, they buried it and the cloth is still bloody, and always will be.[17]

In many ways, St Catherine of Alexandria (not to be confused with the later fourteenth-century St Catherine of Siena) appears to have embodied and foreshadowed the ideals and characteristics of many young, educated, noble virgins who came after her and succeeded to sainthood, or at least developed large followings. Living in the highly volatile times of the Christian persecutions, Catherine had converted to Christianity after a vision as a teenager. She then elected to challenge the many pagan philosophers of her age in an attempt to convert them also, employing her famed intellectual and persuasive rhetoric for the task.

Understandably, Catherine was not always received favourably and hers were dangerous times in which to be openly teaching and disseminating Christianity. However, undeterred she obtained an audience with the Roman emperor Maximus and counselled him on his folly in the worship of false, pagan gods. The furious emperor had Catherine scourged and imprisoned. Catherine came to represent a serious threat to the emperor for she had already swayed the minds of his scholars and then that of his wife, who had converted to Christianity after having felt compelled to visit Catherine in her cell. It was then that Maximus ordered what became the failed attempt at Catherine's execution on her famed wheel and after which she was beheaded.

The endorsement of Catherine's teachings and conversion of pagan minds through the persuasive power of her rhetoric was founded, as was to be the case with many other mystics and visionaries after her, on the reports of her guided visions and visitations from both Christ and the Virgin Mary. Most significantly, she had pronounced herself the appointed earthly spouse of Christ. Early accounts of Catherine's life are few until a Life of her was written in the tenth century. With the removal of some of her relics from Mount Sinai to Rouen (purportedly three of her fingers), came a revival of her cult in the eleventh century. It is also in this century that we discover the first recorded appearance of St Catherine's name in England, within a calendar produced at Winchester, further endorsement of her saintly status in England.[18]

Rouen became the centre for devotion to St Catherine in the west and her legend spread in varying forms and languages. It was her relics, though, as with those of so many saints that served to endorse her legend and their more accessible relocation to Rouen allowed her popularity to become more widespread. With the enactment of miracles said to be generated by the relics came further justification in the medieval mind for reverence to be paid to St Catherine. The bones held at Sinai and Rouen were also said to exude a healing oil which, as with the purported holy blood, breath and tears that constituted some of the holy relics of Christ, was vigilantly collected in phials.

Between the thirteenth and sixteenth centuries, many chapels and churches across western Europe were dedicated to St Catherine. In a literal interpretation of the original resting place of St Catherine on the top of Mount Sinai, many such chapels came to be located on top of hills or mounds. These would have housed cult images of St

Catherine that could be invoked in the same way as her relics at Sinai or at Rouen. Today, one such surviving example of the fourteenth-century devotion to her can still be visited at Abbotsbury in Dorset.

For female devotees, Catherine had become associated with the role of marriage broker, which won her a large following among younger, lower-class women. It is unclear how such an association came to be established, but it saw women invoking her help to find appropriate husbands and may have been connected with her status as a mystical bride of Christ, as with some other virgin saints such as St Bridget or Bride. Hence, on St Catherine's feast day in particular, on 25 November, women would climb to her chapels to invoke her help in finding a suitable match:

> A husband, St Catherine,
> A handsome one, St Catherine,
> A rich one, St Catherine,
> A nice one, St Catherine,
> And soon, St Catherine.[19]

At St Catherine's Chapel in Abbotsbury, Dorset, it became customary for women to place their knees into one hole and their hands in two others in the door jamb. At Catherine chapels with a well, pilgrims would also be able to drink some of the holy water before entering the chapel. Catherine also acquired significant status as a pinnacle of femininity, educated and courteous in her earthly existence and hence in her sainthood equally popular with high-born women. The impact of her short life and her violent end led some to name her as one of the heavenly voices by which Joan of Arc was advised. Today, she is considered the patron of various professions and learned institutions – of libraries and teachers on account of her own learning and intellect, of lawyers on account of her skills of persuasion and debate, and of all craftsmen whose work involves a wheel, such as potters or spinners.

Another mystic and self-proclaimed bride of Christ was to find her faith at a similarly young age, in her native country of Sweden. St Birgitta, Bride or Bridget of Sweden (d. 1373) was a popular saint who in her lifetime displayed a fond attachment to the Virgin in her form of worship and ascetic piety. Much idolised by Margery Kempe in the fifteenth-century account of the latter's pilgrimages, Bridget is said to have experienced a symbolic union with Christ after the death of her husband, in which she believed that Christ had appointed her his spiritual bride. Bridget emulated Mary in her everyday life to the extent that she even reported a mystical pregnancy, believing that she could sense the quickening of a baby inside her – Bridget's symbolic manifestation of the entry of Christ into her heart. She also claimed that the Virgin appeared to her on Christmas Day to reassure her that what she had experienced was a re-creation of the Virgin's own joy at the divine conception and birth of the Christ child. Bridget believed herself the earthly ambassador and instrument of revelation of Christ and the Virgin and the medium through which they would impart their wisdom and counsel as to the ways in which she could improve the spiritual observance of the world.

She professed herself to be guided through visions, dreams and apparitions, accounts of which were later collected and circulated as her *Revelaciones*. On one such occasion Bridget interpreted a call from God to plant a new vineyard as a direction to found a new religious order. This she did in veneration of the Virgin, establishing the beginnings of the Brigittine Order. It was with this instruction that Bridget undertook her pilgrimage to Rome to request permission from the Pope to found the order.

Bridget also held very firm moral opinions including those on the state of marriage, which she believed was for the sole purpose of procreation. Surveying contemporary society and the reasons for marriage, she found much to disappoint: 'The people of this time get married for seven reasons. The first is a beautiful face. The second is extensive possessions. . . . In the seventh place they couple like horses because of frivolous and voluptuous desires.'[20]

Bridget herself had had eight children by her late husband. During her pregnancies they abstained from any sexual contact in order to reaffirm that the sole purpose of their union was indeed procreation.[21] Some devout women became 'vowesses' or took a vow of chastity in the presence of a bishop when they became widowed. However, after the birth of her own children, Margery Kempe made the decision in her husband's lifetime to abstain from sexual relations with him, wishing to become chaste again in her pursuit of holiness and, quite possibly, in emulation of her ideal, Bridget of Sweden. Margaret Beaufort, mother of Henry VII, was another who chose to take a vow of chastity, in her case during the lifetime of her third husband.

On Bridget's death, her daughter Catherine became Superior of the Brigittines, taking up her mother's causes, supporting Pope Urban VI against the antipope, Clement VII in Avignon, and promoting her mother's canonisation. Those women who elected to follow Bridget's doctrine and way of life likewise aspired to emulate the virtues of the Mother of God with whom they believed Bridget to have held private counsel through her visitations. In the light of the popularity of the Marian cult in the Middle Ages, Bridget's status was enhanced as a real person who had managed to achieve a parallel, spiritual, path in life as a beneficiary of her divine revelations and she perhaps represented the physical, corporeal proof and inspiration that other women needed. She was an accessible figure – mother of eight children, a wife and a widow.

The Brigittine Order spread far and wide, a factor in the long-distance range of St Bridget's curative effects. Accounts of the 138 miracles attributed to her powers collected between 1373 and 1390, show that 87 per cent record cures at long distance by beneficiaries who had not necessarily visited her religious centre in Sweden. Simultaneously, this encouraged the establishment of subsidiary shrines dedicated to Bridget in many other parts of Europe.

St Mary Magdalene and her shrine at Vézelay was of particular significance and another female figurehead with whom medieval women would have been well acquainted. Most memorably, she is believed to have been the first to witness the risen Lord when he appeared to her in the garden of his burial. Blinded by tears, she mistook him for the gardener. More recent Western traditions have also linked Mary Magdalene with Mary, the sister of Martha and Lazarus in Bethany and, most influentially, with the sinner in Luke's gospel who washed Christ's feet with her tears and dried them with her hair, an image that has had an enduring influence in Western iconographic traditions. Mary Magdalene has come to be regarded as the patron saint of repentant sinners and the contemplative life.

In the Middle Ages Mary Magdalene's cult was centred on the ninth-century Benedictine abbey of Vézelay in France. By the eleventh century, the monks at Vézelay were claiming ownership of relics associated with Mary Magdalene, purportedly brought back from the Holy Land by their founder St Badilo. In order to support the unsubstantiated claim that Mary Magdalene's remains were indeed interred in their abbey church, the monks devised and circulated a legend. It told that after Christ's death, Mary Magdalene had set sail for exile in France to gain absolution for her sins. When she died she was buried in the town known today as St Maximin la Sainte-Baume, but in the eighth century her remains were moved to Vézelay. In turn, this transformed Vézelay from what had been a quiet backwater in a corner of Burgundy into a powerful and affluent monastery, a rise to fame paralleled by several other previously obscure religious centres that subsequently achieved acclaim and wealth on account of their relics.[22] An altar to Mary Magdalene, the prototype of the penitent, was erected with railings to protect it; where pilgrims could come and offer their supplications and prayers to their saint. Vézelay's abbey stood at the beginning of one of the four main pilgrimage trails leading to the cathedral of St James of Compostela in north-west Spain, so that it also received large numbers of visitors who were en route. So great was the shrine's popularity that it was not long before a new abbey church, dedicated on 21 April 1104, had to be erected in order to accommodate the influx of pilgrims. Later, an enclosed porch, or narthex, for pilgrims was added.

In the genre of hagiographical compendia, a Life of Mary Magdalene was compiled in 1260 by Jacobus de Voragine, an Italian Dominican and author of the *Legenda Aurea*. According to the *Legenda*, the adoration of St Mary Magdalene at Vézelay was accompanied by many miracles. She is supposed to have brought a dead knight to life and restored the sight to a blind pilgrim when he entreated her help in front of the church of Vézelay. She was also said to have released a prisoner from chains and to have shown the path of virtue to a sinful priest.

However, Vézelay's fortunes began to wane in the thirteenth century. Disputes within the monastery along with its diminishing wealth began to take their toll. It seems that the monks of St Maximin saw this as a golden opportunity to reclaim what they felt to be rightfully theirs. What followed was that Mary's relics were 'rediscovered' in the crypt of St Maximin and the discovery duly announced on 9 December 1279. The fact that King Louis and the papal legate had earlier proclaimed Vézelay's relics authentic in 1267 was an incongruous, but not altogether uncommon event amid the frenzy that was the medieval relic trade. The monks of St Maximin endorsed their find with the simultaneous unearthing of an inscription verifying the authenticity of their relics. The way in which the new relics of Mary Magdalene were readily venerated and those at Vézelay consigned to distant memory is illuminating as regards the workings of the medieval psyche where holy relics were concerned. Pilgrims were quickly drawn to the Provençal shrine and happily made their supplications to Mary Magdalene at the new shrine and no questions asked as to the apparent miracle working of her relics at Vézelay, whether they had been false all along, or whether Vézelay had in fact been in possession of the relics of *another* miracle-working saint. All was lost for Vézelay.

In the second half of the twelfth century, the shrine of Our Lady of Rocamadour, to the north-west of Conques, developed an international reputation as a centre of devotion to the Virgin Mary, drawing pilgrims from Spain, Italy, Germany, England and the Latin East as well as France. Requiring a rather rocky detour, the shrine was found on a cliff reached by flights of steps. Its popularity was attested to in the 126 miracle stories recorded there between 1172 and 1173. Reflecting and enhancing Rocamadour's status was the varying nature of the illnesses, injuries and predicaments that pilgrims brought to the shrine in hope of intercession by the Virgin. Among those who received cures were a woman afflicted by many blows, a woman who went into labour every day, the deaf, the blind, those with dropsy, a mute woman to whom the power of speech was restored and a woman cured of a polyp.

Rocamadour was also popular with the aristocracy being visited by Simon de Montfort and Henry II, among others. Indeed, the peak of Rocamadour's fame coincided with the year of Thomas Becket's martyrdom in 1170 when England's king Henry II chose to make a pilgrimage there. A fascinating feature of the shrine was its liberal scattering of tufts and locks of hair. While an awe-inspiring sight, the significance of this gesture by pilgrims would have been understood. The most popular legend relating to the shrine speaks of a woman afflicted with blindness as a result of her lascivious life-style. Her sight was restored when she came to Rocamadour and she duly offered up her thanksgiving to the Virgin. Before the woman could enter the sanctuary, though, she was ordered by the priest to cut off her long hair in honour of the Virgin. As with the tresses of many women before her, her hair was cut, carried into the church and displayed as a reminder to all women saved from personal vanity by the Virgin's grace. However, on leaving the sanctuary the woman began to lament her decision and mourned her lost hair. In an instant, her hair was returned to her head, and blindness to her eyes.

One of Edward II's yeomen, Gerald Donum, went on pilgrimage to the church of St Mary Rocamadour, in his case to fulfil a vow he had made when his life had been in danger at sea. He also pledged to maintain his beard until he reached Rocamadour where he would cut it and leave it at the church as a symbol of his salvation at the hands of the Virgin.[23]

There were many other saints within the female litany who are less well known today and perhaps enjoyed less of a cult status in the Middle Ages, but who nevertheless received the recognition and invocations of pilgrims at smaller shrines across Britain. These included the shrines of St Winifrede's Well, St Etheldreda at Ely and St Candida at Whitchurch Canonicorum, Dorset. That is not to say that these saints were any less important. Each had their own functions and associations as intercessory saints and at whose shrines petitioning pilgrims would arrive with their incantations and hearts hopeful of gaining saintly intervention.

NINE

Pitstops and Provision — Catering for the Woman Pilgrim

the poor hospital of Canterbury, commonly called 'Estbruge' founded by Saint Thomas the Martyr, for the poor, for persons going to Rome . . . and for lying-in [pregnant] women.

As with modern travel, much of the pilgrim's journey and experience could depend on their personal circumstances, for example whether they were able to travel in relative luxury with a large retinue and the resources to pay for comfortable lodgings en route, or whether they had to rely on hospitality and charity. These concerns were coupled with other influential factors including the weather, the kind of companions you fell in with along the way, whether you had the misfortune to be robbed or caught up in a storm at sea, or became ill. Some help was available. There were provisions made along the way for the care and sustenance of the pilgrim on their sacred path. Such provision was aimed at the pilgrim *per se*, rather than there being any specific arrangement for women, men, or those travelling with children. However, study of surviving accounts indicates that the experience of male and female pilgrims could be quite different so that with time, some gender-specific arrangements were introduced and certain concessions won through the persistence and resourcefulness of women pilgrims themselves.

The pilgrim was a common figure throughout Europe during the Middle Ages and was easily recognised by their pilgrim garb. The key elements of this dress were a scrip or small satchel and a staff to assist walking, for example up hills or across water, or even for use in self-defence. The scrip could contain small provisions as well as his letter of commendation, or *testimoniales*, permission to go on the pilgrimage and granted either by his feudal lord, bishop or abbot, as well as proof of his identity as a *bona fide* pilgrim. The staff might also serve as an implement from which to hang a drinking flask and often ended in two prongs. St James of Compostela, who became the patron saint of pilgrims, is often depicted thus – staff in hand and with scrip at his hip.

It was the scallop shell that became the best-known symbol of both pilgrimage and pilgrim, its origin derived from the shrine of St James and its associated mythology on the north-west coast of Spain where pilgrims originally gathered their scallop shell souvenirs. A pilgrim's hat is also mentioned in literature, pilgrim accounts and imagery, often with a brim broad enough to act as a sun shield and allow the attachment of lead souvenir badges from each of the shrines a pilgrim visited. Together with the trademark long cloak for warmth and perhaps for use as a blanket, and boots, all of these items appeared in contemporary literature, both sacred and secular. For example, when Reynard the Fox wishes to disguise himself as a pilgrim we are told: 'Reynard now sees that this is what he must do. He takes a scrip and staff and sets out on his way, looking every inch a pilgrim.'[1]

Along with the recommended blessing and attire of the pilgrim came the mystical bestowal of pilgrim status on the individual who was forsaking home and the familiar for a sacred journey, in devotional heart to a chosen or prescribed site of religious veneration. Having assumed this role, the pilgrim was entitled to hostelry and alms on the journey, as well as certain other concessions. For example, the *licentia Romani pontificis* which commended pilgrims to make the journey to the Holy Land also accorded them certain benefits, such as exemption from criminal or civil suits brought against them in their absence, stays of any such suits that involved debt, as well as access to special facilities for loans.

With regard to the paths followed by the pilgrim, many routes became well established, particularly those to the larger, most popular shrines. The London–Canterbury and Winchester–Canterbury routes became well-trodden paths followed by several pilgrim bands. For those three most prestigious overseas destinations, Rome, Santiago de Compostela and the Holy Land, there were also customary routes and modes of transport for the pilgrim. Santiago de Compostela, for example, was the object of four main routes that led across France and the Pyrénées to its location in north-west Spain. The most westerly path began at Tours in the Loire Valley. This well-provisioned route extended south through the Bordeaux region, offering the easiest terrain, but the longest expedition. A second path commenced at Vézelay in Burgundy, leading the pilgrim across the centre of France through Bourges and Limoges. Pilgrims on this route would stop at the Church of St Marie Magdalene in Vézelay in order to view its holy relics.[2]

From the third starting point, that at Le Puy, the pilgrim was set on the Via Podiensis, which passed though Conques and Moissac. At Le Puy stood the Hospital of St Mary dedicated to Our Lady of Le Puy and in the abbey church at Conques a spectacular reliquary of the early Gallic martyr St Faith drew in many pilgrims. Rocamadour, to the north-west of Conques, was also popular with pilgrims. The fourth route, beginning at Arles, near the mouth of the

Rhône, assumed a westward path to Santiago and passed through Toulouse. This route was most convenient for pilgrims who had journeyed south from the direction of Aachen, Cologne and Trier in Germany. Cologne, one of the noted sites of the Wife of Bath's impressive itinerary, attracted many pilgrims of its own on account of its shrine to the Three Kings.

Aside from offering many side trips and points of interest, these four paths were also well served by hostelries. In the eleventh century, St Domingo de la Calzada devoted himself to the founding of pilgrims' hostels and the improvement of pilgrim roads and bridges. At the height of Compostela's popularity as a pilgrimage destination, from the twelfth to the fourteenth century, hostels were conveniently located within a day's walk of each other, and modern-day pilgrims can still benefit from the provision of *refugios* along the way.[3]

Those pilgrims to Rome from England would begin with their sea journey to the Continent and then link up with one of the established routes, the Via Francigena used by tradesmen, merchants, ecclesiastics and pilgrims travelling from north-western Europe to Rome. This journey involved the sometimes treacherous crossing of the Alps, often at the mercy of the weather, and was usually undertaken via the Mont Cenis or the Mont Joux further north (Mons Jovis, later called the Great St Bernard). At the summit of Mont Cenis, the pilgrims might rest and refresh themselves at an abbey dedicated to St Peter and a ninth-century hospice before their descent into northern Italy. The Great and Little St Bernard Passes were named in honour and memory of the charitable work of Bernard of Aosta in the region of the Alps. A twelfth-century letter from one pilgrim who made the strenuous journey gives a picture of the conditions such pilgrims might encounter:

Forgive my not writing, I have been on the Mons Jovis [Great Bernard] . . . I put my hand in my scrip to scratch out a word or two to your sincerity; behold I found my ink bottle filled with a dry mass of ice. My fingers refused to write; my beard was stiff with frost, and my breath congealed in a long icicle. I could not write.[4]

For those pilgrims setting out on the longest and most strenuous journeys, the Holy Land presented the greatest challenge. After a stop at Venice to pick up their sea passage, pilgrims would spend most of their journey at sea in the squalid conditions of a pilgrim galley. Perhaps the most poignant and enlightening accounts that we have of pilgrim experiences while en route relate to sea journeys and the storms, shipwrecks, drownings and sickness that occurred.

The voyage from Venice took the pilgrims across a long stretch of the Mediterranean Sea to Jaffa. It could include stops at any of the Mediterranean islands (with their own growing repertoire of venerated sites and native saints) in order to stock up on provisions and fresh water. Saewulf's itinerary mentions stops at the islands of Corfu, Cephalonia, Crete and Samos to name but four. However, plague or ill weather at sea could also prevent a vessel from dropping anchor at a port.

The advice of one fifteenth-century pilgrim guidebook to the Holy Land counselled the pilgrim to choose his place on board the galley with some care, in order at least to limit some of the symptoms of storm and sickness at sea: 'as nyghe the myddes of the shippe as ye may, for there is leest rollynge or tomblinge to kepe your brayne and stomache in temper . . .'.[5] From Jaffa, pilgrims would be under the supervision of their Saracen guides and begin their ride across the desert, by ass, to Jerusalem.

Some of the earliest known hostelries for pilgrims were provided by the Church or individual monasteries. Monasteries and people in the villages along the pilgrim ways were encouraged to offer them hospitality; in so doing, they were deemed to share in the merit, virtue and spiritual reward of the pilgrim's sacred journey, assisting them with a bed for the night, or with some sustenance. Monasteries were to provide this service free to the pilgrim in a similar manner to giving alms to the poor, and some were even advised to set aside part of their revenue for this purpose. Monastic houses in the vicinity of larger, more established shrines were more likely to play host to the richer pilgrim of noble or gentry status. In such instances, some form of payment for their stay was encouraged in order to support the monastic house concerned. This seemingly fair arrangement came undone, however, when monastic houses gave the wealthier visitor preferential treatment over the poorer, more needy pilgrim, to satisfy their own material interest. This was an unfortunate reality, especially as pilgrimage became a money-making industry in its own right, with profit to be made in several quarters.

For the devout or needy pilgrim, though, monasteries were a particularly favoured option, given that they were often equipped with their own infirmary so that those pilgrims in need of medical attention and their guests could receive physical as well as spiritual care. Here pilgrims would be fed as well as given a blessing before once more departing on their way. A halt at a monastery might serve as a reaffirmation of the pilgrim's purpose as a servant of God, setting out on his pious journey to repair the moral order of his or her life, receive forgiveness for sin and commend their soul to the Lord. Monastic establishments were able to supply spiritual sustenance, as well as food and a bed for the night. The Cluniac monasteries in particular were noted for their hospitality to pilgrims.

For those pilgrims who could afford it, there were also taverns and inns close by many of the larger shrines where they might enjoy a hot meal and a more comfortable bed, that is if the latter was not infested with fleas or to be shared with other pilgrims. The Tabard Inn in Southwark is where Chaucer has the pilgrims meet in his *Canterbury Tales* and in an Epilogue to the tales the Chequer of Hope is mentioned, the largest of Canterbury's inns, situated on the corner of the High Street and Mercery Lane, which would have been lined with the stalls of souvenir vendors. The Chequer of Hope was built by Christ Church Priory between 1392 and 1395 at a cost of £867 14s 4d and some of the original façade is still visible.

Chaucer's pilgrims stayed here on their arrival in the city, the inn's name being a corruption of the chessboard on the hoop, or barrel:

> They toke hir In, and loggit hem and mydmorowe, I trowe,
> Atte 'Cheker of the hope', yat many a man doith knowe. . . .[6]

As it did with the lodgings, taverns and inns on pilgrim routes, the level of hospitality offered by monasteries or other religious houses could vary. Among those noted for their hospitality to pilgrims was the Guesten Hall at Canterbury. Here, as a result of statutes laid down by Archbishop Winchelsea, pilgrim guests were entitled to a meal of meat and bread each day, as well as to the privilege of burial within the grounds of Christ Church if they should happen to die there, regardless of status or birth. The Cathedral of St James of Compostela in Spain had been granted land by the city's archbishop, Gelmirez, specifically for the burial of pilgrims. At the time of Abbot Agelwy in the eleventh century pilgrims to Evesham Abbey could be the beneficiaries of his own particular brand of charity – in a re-enactment of Christ's washing of his disciples' feet, the Abbot bathed the feet of pilgrims. Evidence suggests that this was a procedure encouraged for such clerics, but not one that was widely practised.

As a major pilgrimage centre, Canterbury also had other provision for the pilgrim in the form of two hospitals. One of these, the Hospital of St Nicholas situated a mile outside the city at Harbledown, had been founded by Archbishop Lanfranc in 1084. In the Middle Ages the term 'hospital' described a hospitable institution for the benefit of the pilgrim or *hospes* (Latin 'guest') and the needy, as well as one that cared for the sick. At St Nicholas's Hospital, pilgrims were welcome to take water at the holy well, to kiss its holy relics, but of particular interest was the hospital's association with those visitors afflicted with leprosy. On account of the leprosy, the floor was set at an angle to allow the building to be flushed out and cleaned after the lepers had attended mass. On his penitential crawl to the Canterbury shrine after his barons murdered of Thomas

Becket, Henry II was recorded as having made a stop at the hospital at Harbledown.

Such hospitals were sometimes founded by religious orders, such as the Knights Templar who were recognised guardians of the pilgrim and the traveller, as well as by other fraternities, perhaps of importance and with the means to underwrite such an undertaking. Commanderies were also set up by other orders of knights for the same purpose. Of these some still survive, such as the National Trust house at Sutton-at-Hone, Dartford, formerly a commandery of the Knights of St John of Jerusalem. The grandson of William the Conqueror, Henry of Blois, founded a charitable foundation outside Winchester in 1136 known as the Hospital of St Cross. It consisted of a large hall in which pilgrims could eat and sleep as well as having its own chapel. In 1445, the Almshouse of Noble Poverty was added; it still accommodates twenty-five brothers who live in its fifteenth-century quarters.

Perhaps the most famous hospice was the Hospital of St John the Baptist set up in Jerusalem. Having become the headquarters of a crusading order after the capture of Jerusalem in the First Crusade of 1095, it continued to operate as a hospice, apparently with extensive accommodation and generous provision for the pilgrim and the sick. In his thirteenth-century description of the Holy Land's sites Theoderich tells us:

> no one can credibly tell another how beautiful its buildings are, how abundantly it is supplied with rooms and beds and other material for the use of poor and sick people, how rich it is in the means of refreshing the poor, and how devotedly it labors to maintain the needy, unless one has the opportunity of seeing it with one's own eyes . . . we saw that the beds numbered more than one thousand . . .[7]

Although we cannot be certain of the accuracy of Theoderich's description, it is certain that a great many laymen and pilgrims would have passed through the hospice's doors in a week, since it was the largest and most well-known establishment for pilgrims in Jerusalem. Clerics would stay at the Franciscan community on Mount Sion.

In Canterbury itself was the Eastbridge Hospital or St Thomas's Hospital as it is also known. Still open to visitors today, it incorporates the earliest part of the building, its Undercroft, where the pilgrims would have slept, a refectory with minstrels' gallery and a pilgrims' chapel. It was founded by Archbishop Walter (1193–1205) and by 1342 it was said to have a total of twelve beds, eight for men and four for women, the provision of the hospice being expounded by Archbishop Stratford as: 'for the maintenance of poor pilgrims and other infirm persons resorting thither to remain until they are healed of their infirmities; for the poor, persons going to Rome, for others coming to Canterbury and needing shelter. . . .'[8]

The eighth and ninth centuries had seen a marked increase in the number of hospices in response to increased travel and by the twelfth century came a clearer differentiation between earlier charitable institutions and hospitals for the pilgrim *hospes* or guest, and those other guesthouses, inns or taverns providing board and lodging. Hospices were institutions that needed to secure a regular income and generally relied upon donations, legacies and bequests. As the pilgrim routes and shrines became more established and the practice of pilgrimage more popular, such hospices sprang up conveniently along the many pilgrim trails.

Hospices were founded for a variety of reasons, from the reverential to the charitable, even as an expression of thanksgiving. For example, a hospice at Aubrac was founded in 1100 by a Flemish nobleman to give thanks for his safe return to Santiago de Compostela after being caught in a threatening blizzard. Those three hostels mentioned as of particular note in a guidebook for pilgrims to St James's shrine in Spain, the *Liber Sancti Jacobi* were that at Jerusalem, the Great St Bernard Pass and that of St Christine in the Pyrénées, all strategically placed to cater for pilgrims to the main pilgrimage centres. The Great St Bernard Pass in the Alps stood at its bleakest and most exposed point and had been founded by Bernard of Aosta for the benefit of pilgrims travelling towards Rome. The Hospice of St Christine was positioned on the Somport Pass over the Pyrénées, frequented by pilgrims on their way to Santiago de Compostela. On another principal pass over the Pyrénées was another, twelfth-century hospice, founded by the Bishop of Pamplona at Roncesvalles.

Sometimes, specific provision was made for women pilgrims, but not often, so that those venues that did so are sometimes accorded special mention. One of the aspects of the Eastbridge Hospital in Canterbury that related directly to women concerned the provision made for 'lying-in women', or those about to give birth. There is evidence that women did undergo pilgrimage while they were pregnant, presumably sometimes as a *result* of being pregnant in order to make appropriate supplications for a safe labour and delivery. Otherwise, women might conceive while away on pilgrimage, or else set out unaware that they were pregnant. Margaret of Beverley in Yorkshire was apparently conceived in England just prior to her parents' departure on a pilgrimage to Jerusalem, where she was subsequently born in 1155. More extraordinarily, Margaret returned to Jerusalem in 1187 when it was besieged by Saladin, during which episode she sported a breastplate and set a cauldron on her head for a helmet and joined the fray.

Another larger establishment of this type was based in the Holy Land. Such were the directives written by Roger de Moulins in 1181 for the Hospital of St John in Jerusalem:

> It is also decreed that little cradles should be made for the babies of women pilgrims born in the House, so that they may lie separate, and that the baby in its own bed may be in no danger from the restlessness of its mother.[9]

The order of the Knights Hospitallers prescribed a mode of conduct for all their members in respect of the treatment of pregnant women and even the care of their newborn babies. The works of St James of Pistoia appeared to advocate similar consideration, and note the case of one woman who gave birth to a boy at the hospital there who was given alms to the sum of £1 12*s*. Families might also be the recipients of such almsgiving and the same list includes a poor man, his wife and their five children all bound on pilgrimage.

Aside from such occasional provision made for pregnant women and the delivery of babies while their mothers were on pilgrimage, more common was the arrangement made at hostels for the separation of men from women, something of which Margery Kempe would probably have wholeheartedly approved. The proprietor at Piacenza saw fit to make special provision for women pilgrims by building a separate annexe to lodge them. The very nature of pilgrimage created a more fluid, transitional existence for people from all levels of society and of both sexes than was common in this period, uniting them in a common cause, so that pilgrims from every walk of life were thrown together in a mélange of sexes, ages and class. Felix Fabri's account testifies to how this intermingling could sometimes engender class tension – when, for example, and as mentioned earlier, some disgruntled young noblemen on the way to receive their knighthoods were forced to share their sea passage with some equally feisty old widows.

Pilgrimage also allowed for greater freedom of movement and interaction between the sexes and by the time that criticism of pilgrimage practice was reaching its height in the fourteenth century, sexual indiscretions and lasciviousness were noted issues of contention. Much has been written about the medieval pilgrim as a transient, displaced individual, someone who finds themself living outside the constraints of their ordinary life, in a state of temporary instability and tasting adventure probably for the first time. It is described as a situation in which all things became possible, new friendships and bonds were forged and an examination of one's own character and limitations could be prompted by the hardships endured and the new experiences pilgrimage afforded. One scholar recounts how pilgrims away from home formed their own 'community in which class and gender are *less* significant; they have removed themselves from the influences of power, place and time of their societies'.[10] Many monastic houses reacted by arranging a respectful segregation of the sexes which might well include the separation of husbands and wives, as at the Hospital of St John in Jerusalem.

In some cases, the provision of separate accommodation for women pilgrims became necessary where none had existed before. In the Holy Land, for example, Brother Felix Fabri explains how two Latin monasteries alongside the Church of the Holy Sepulchre were established to cater for the large numbers of pilgrims flocking to the sacred site:

> They therefore built a monastery in honour of the blessed Virgin Mary in front of the door of the Church of the Holy Sepulchre, and placed therein an abbot and Latin monks . . . they called the place itself St Mary the Latin. . . . As a multitude of pilgrims flowed thither, both men and women, the men were received into the guest-house of the monastery, but the women lodged without its walls, as best they could, and sometimes they were molested by the Saracens and suffered loss thereby. So the monks, after calling upon Mary the helper of pilgrims to aid them, built, near their own monastery, against the wall of the Church of the Holy Sepulchre, another monastery for women on the left hand as one enters the church, which was called St Mary Magdalen's, wherein women pilgrims were received and well treated.'[11]

Fabri made two pilgrimages to the Holy Land in the fourteenth century and relates for a second time the creation of the separate monastery for female pilgrims, '. . . owing to the numbers of women pilgrims who came thither, another monastery was built, wherein women pilgrims were lodged'. He also noted how ever-increasing multitudes of pilgrims flocked to the Sepulchre so that such monasteries struggled to house them.

It seems that the order of knights in charge of the Sepulchre shrine had become less rigid in terms of receiving pilgrim guests of both sexes and all classes. In a eulogy to the knighthood of the Holy Sepulchre, Brother Fabri commended it as the 'best and noblest of all knighthood'. One of the reasons he gives for this is that while other knights would not demean themselves by mixing with anyone other than those of noble birth, this order of knighthood rejected no one, regardless of class or sex, their members travelling across the sea to Jerusalem alongside beggars as well as monks and merchants:

> nay, they even cross in company with women, both young and old; with Beguines and nuns, and heed not the foolish sneers of their detractors, who say that the Knighthood of the Holy Sepulchre is womanish, because of the old women in whose company it is gained.[12]

As pilgrim numbers increased and many monasteries struggled to house them, so new building projects were undertaken to provide the extra accommodation required. This was the case at Worcester Cathedral, for example, the remains of its Guesten Hall being still visible in the cathedral grounds. The Strangers' Hall built during the reign of Edward I (1272–1307) was erected by the monks of St Swithun's Priory, Winchester, in order to receive pilgrim guests visiting the shrine there.

Another aspect of pilgrimage provision for women concerned access to certain holy sites from which their sex ordinarily excluded them but which they might nevertheless visit by employing a measure of resourcefulness and persistence. For example, women were not permitted to enter monastery precincts and would find their way barred by the marking of a boundary. Naturally, where holy relics were housed within a monastery, this would normally prevent them from gaining access. However, in one recorded instance at St Benoît at Fleury,[13] the women were left standing at the monastery gates while the men processed inside to view the holy relics. However, after much wrangling and pleading, a pavilion was erected outside to which the relics were conveyed and temporarily displayed.

A similar event occurred at Pontigny at the shrine to St Edmund, former Archbishop of Canterbury, which had become increasingly popular as news of its miracle-working spread.[14] The shrine was a particular favourite of women devotees, which immediately presented a problem since it was situated within a monastery. On this occasion, rather than permit access to the women who had flocked to Pontigny the monks decided to bring the saint to them – in the form of his arm, duly brought out to the women pilgrims waiting at the monastery gates. It is interesting that the decision to dismember the arm from the rest of the saint's remains is taken partly to avoid dampening the women's fervour and devotion by barring them from viewing the saint, and partly to secure the revenue that their devotions brought in the form of offerings. Thus, the monks resourcefully observed the customs of their shrine while benefiting from the 'no small income from the women's offerings'.[15] However, it is also mentioned, perhaps as a note of caution, that the division of the saint's remains in this way had displeased both God and the saint, to the extent that his relics would not perform miracles thereafter, or at least not in public.

The shrine of St Edmund of Canterbury at Pontigny is also mentioned in a letter of 1255, this time from the priest of San Lorenzo in Lucina to the abbot and convent of Pontigny. The letter suggests that the influx of women pilgrims to the shrine could be better accommodated by allowing them access to the chapter room of the monastery where they might make their supplications and offer up prayers to the saints. However, this measure should only be adopted if they were accompanied by other women of good repute and on the basis that the women pilgrims had come in pure and devotional spirit. However, women pilgrims would not be allowed to eat or sleep within the confines of the monastery. Again, the reason given for such a concession is the greater glory of St Edmund as well as the furthering of the devotions of his suppliants, but there can be no doubt that the monks and church authorities knew they could ill afford to forfeit gifts and offerings of so many women pilgrims. Not least, such a scenario underlines the importance of the financial contribution made by women pilgrims to the pilgrimage industry.

In 1243, Pope Innocent IV had made a similar concession to the Queen of England, Eleanor of Provence, granting her leave to enter monasteries in England stipulating only that she do so in the company of ten good and honest women and enter the churches and cloisters for the purpose of prayer.[16] The shrine or feretory of St Cuthbert in Durham Cathedral was another area to which women were normally forbidden access, here on account of the saint's apparent misogyny. This embargo, however, served to bolster the popularity of the neighbouring shrine of St Frideswide (see Chapter 8).

From Brother Fabri's account of his second voyage to the Holy Land it is possible to infer the existence of restrictions on women aboard ship. He details the arrangements for eating and sleeping and the food supplied to the pilgrims, while noting also that 'women pilgrims do not come to the common table, but remain in their berths, and both eat and sleep there . . .'. Whether this situation existed out of the women's own choice or whether it was due to a requirement that women remain in their berths for eating and sleeping is not stated, but the fact that it is mentioned at all appears significant. The usually squalid, stifling conditions below decks on pilgrim galleys were well documented and, as Fabri matter of factly states, 'In stormy weather eating and vomiting go on at the same time . . .'. It seems unlikely, then, that women would have elected to confine themselves in such conditions.

Part of the rationale for prohibiting women to enter certain shrines was deeply embedded in the medieval psyche and had its roots in the biblical teaching of the sins of Eve and hence the belief, found through Christendom, in women's inherent lasciviousness and even their potential to taint holy relics and sacred spaces by association. The volatile and emotional tendencies of women are also cited as a potentially disruptive force. In this context, in his description of the monks of St Catherine's monastery, Felix Fabri recounts how

> Their buildings, as I have told you, are in no ways admirable or costly. I lay in the cell of one of the ancient Fathers, and saw therein nought save signs of extreme poverty. No woman enters into them, neither are pilgrim women from overseas parts let in, if they come thither, for the monks know the bitter jest:
>
> > To the place where women dwell,
> > Peace and quiet bid farewell;
> > Never can they both contrive
> > Underneath one roof to thrive.
> > He that lives a single life,
> > He alone lives without strife . . .
>
> not to speak of the numberless other perils which monks incur by dwelling together with women, to all of which they give due weight, and suffer no woman to approach them.[17]

Fortunately, such misogyny was even then not universal. Some religious houses recognised the abundant benefits to be had from allowing women devotees to visit their shrines, some thus even permitting access to women where it had previously been denied. Female petitioners at shrines could be powerful agents in reaffirming the popularity and importance of a particular saint or of their miracle-working capacity. Aside from the value of the money and other gifts they bestowed on the houses' holy relics, their disseminating of positive experiences immeasurably assisted in bolstering the prestige of a particular saint, shrine or cult.

Another aspect of pilgrimage that was contingent on the pilgrim's sex concerned the commutation of vows to undertake a pilgrimage. Papal letters provide interesting evidence why some pilgrimages by women required commutation by the Church, most commonly in view of old age or sickness, familial or domestic ties, pregnancy or recent widowhood; and for male and female pilgrims alike, for reasons of war or plague. In the case of one Joanne de Pacy, she was released from her vow on account of her being pregnant every year since she professed her vow. Ironically, she had originally uttered the vow while in the throes of a difficult labour.

A similar case is that of the dispensation granted by Pope John XXII to a French knight and his wife.[18] Having vowed to take a pilgrimage to Compostela when she was gravely ill, the woman found herself unable to fulfil the vow on account of many childbirths (about twenty). Her husband Hugh de Boville made her case to the Bishop of Paris and her vow was commuted into other works of piety. Nor were requests for the commutation of pilgrimage vows confined to women of the lower classes. Elizabeth de Burgh, daughter of Henry Plantagenet, 3rd Earl of Leicester, petitioned the Pope for the transmuting of a vow she had made in her husband's lifetime to go to the Holy Land and Santiago de Compostela, 'which being forty she cannot hope to fulfil'. Her petition was granted.[19]

However, while family matters, old age or ill-health were generally accepted as legitimate reasons for non-completion of vows, other means of fulfilling the vow were usually exacted. For women (if, for example, a proxy pilgrim did not make the journey in their place) this might mean substituting a vow of chastity or else making a donation of the cost of the pilgrimage to the religious building that was to have been their destination.

By dint of their sex, their domestic commitments and respon-sibilities and their perceived vulnerabilities, female pilgrims might thus require both additional provision or dispensation regarding their pilgrimage journeys. We have seen that in some instances such gender-specific requirements were readily catered for in terms of hospitality, with some establishments providing more elaborate accommodation than others, and that there might also be specific provision for women who gave birth within a hostel. In order to prevent the obvious disgrace of Christian women being defiled by Saracens, provision was made for them to stay in safer lodgings. Sometimes, in the face of persistent attempts by women pilgrims to see the holy relics in a monastery, the monks were persuaded for material as well as spiritual reasons to bring the relics to them. However, in no other respect were women the recipients of special concessions on their pilgrimages; normally they must expect the same as the men.

Aside from the possibility of rape, restricted access or of conceiving or delivering a child on the way, in terms of provision, accommodation and safety, the pilgrimage experience was essentially the same for women as it was for men. Those concessions that were granted to women on pilgrimage were motivated either by pious charity, as in the case of the furnishing of cradles for newborn babies, the necessity of accommodating women about to give birth, or the founding of new buildings to house an increasing number of female pilgrims, or out of a desire for profit, as with those monks who give in to the women at the gates of Pontigny or St Benoît. It was generally believed that ultimately God would provide for his pilgrims, so that they need carry with them 'no manner of thing. . . . But meekly ask their meat where they might it get for St Charity', a concept that applied equally to women as to men.[20]

TEN

Hazards and Mishaps – Danger Along the Way

How dangerous it is to lead attractive, nay beautiful young women . . . into foreign parts in quest of indulgences, particularly inexperienced wives . . .[1]

Some of the dangers and difficulties faced by women pilgrims were those of a perennial and gender-specific nature, such as the anxieties for the preservation of her chastity reported by Margery Kempe, who 'dare not sleep any night'. In the memoirs of Arnold von Harff, a well-travelled German pilgrim of the fifteenth century, is included a list of useful phrases, some of which would seem to corroborate Kempe's fears of what some male pilgrims might expect from their female counterparts – such phrases as 'Madam, shall I marry you?', 'Madam, shall I sleep with you?' and 'Good woman, I am already in your bed!'

In accompanying her daughter on a pilgrimage to Rome, the mother of Matilda Montague, an abbess of Barking, cited her concerns for their safety and the necessity for a protective escort for their journey. Unwavering in her faith, Matilda transmuted her fear into the belief that they already had an escort – St John the Evangelist was to be their protective guide. However, it would seem that Matilda's mother's concerns were not without foundation.

In Richard II's reign, one Thomas Walsham, a former canon of Walsingham, was accused of the rape of Emma, wife of William Bole, while she made pilgrimage to Canterbury. He is accused of stealing her goods as well as the money from her purse. Similarly, one Alice Pykemere of Chester was robbed and kidnapped with other pilgrims on her return from Walsingham in 1410. Alice's captors moved her from village to village finally making her swear on the Bible that she would not report them or seek justice for their crimes.

Perhaps most disturbing is the detail of one Isolda Parewastel of Bridgwater. She spent three years in the Holy Land and 'has there been stripped and placed head downwards on a rack, and beaten; then, half dead, she miraculously escaped from the Saracens, and now proposes to build a chapel at Bridgwater in honour of the Blessed Virgin, and for her soul's health . . .'.[2] Isolda petitioned the Pope for permission to build the chapel, which lay in the diocese of Wells. The Pope slightly altered the terms of her petition, granting instead that Isolda be allowed to found an altar in the existing Bridgwater parish church, rather than build a new church. In a separate petition, the Pope also granted that whoever visited the altar on appointed feast days would receive a partial indulgence, pardoning them the standard one year and forty days' penance in Purgatory for their sins. Having survived her ordeal at the hands of the Saracens, Isolda returned home from Jerusalem intent on setting up an altar for the benefit of all comers.

Such instances show that women on pilgrimage were probably subject to greater dangers because of their sex, a situation acknowledged in a Perugian statute of 1343, for example, which stated that women had come to be 'vulnerable and subject to all kinds of insult when visiting the Church of San Domenico in

Perugia'.[3] Also documented is the capture of a woman pilgrim and her husband on their return from a pilgrimage to Rome – their safe delivery from which prompted them to found the priory at Horsham dedicated to St Faith. The Paston letters also recount an instance of a man and woman pilgrim travelling together and coming under attack by robbers. In her letter of 11 March 1450 to John Paston, Agnes writes:

> and they took two pilgrims, a man and a woman, and they robbed the woman, and let her go, and led the man to the sea, and when they knew he was a pilgrim, they gave him money and set him again on the land.[4]

The robber may have felt that the woman was an easier target and less likely to retaliate, and so he robbed her while taking more definite measures against her male companion. Their decision to release him when they discover he is a pilgrim is not as far-fetched as it may seem. Just as it was believed that pilgrims should be offered hospitality and alms as suppliants on a journey of faith, so to attack a pilgrim was perceived as an irreverent act. However, this did not stop pilgrims from being robbed of their money or gifts they were carrying. There were even instances of pilgrims being strip-searched in order to locate any money they might have sewn into their clothes. Furthermore, pilgrims might find themselves subject to much worse treatment at the hands of the Saracens in the Holy Land, for the latter did not recognise any honour in the role of the Latin pilgrim.

Perhaps Margery Kempe best encapsulates the concerns faced by women pilgrims. She has been discouraged from travelling alone with any man on her journey and advised to stay in the company of several other pilgrims at all times. This counsel requires that she decline even the company of a sole friar whom she encounters.

Ironically, those pilgrims of higher birth with their large retinues, protection and provisions for a more comfortable journey could set themselves apart for unwanted attention from vagabonds and thieves. In 1332, Margery de Chaumpaigne went overseas with Eleanor, the sister of Edward II. Four months into their pilgrimage to Santiago de Compostela, they were targeted by robbers who drove away eight of the horses, carried off their goods and assaulted their men and servants.

However, pilgrims it seems were not only the victims of violence but might also be its perpetrators. This is suggested by the apparent necessity inherent in the statutes of Richard I to assign punishments for crimes committed on board ship to the Holy Land:

> if a pilgrim should kill another, he shall be bound to the body of his victim and flung into the sea; that if a pilgrim attack another with a knife or so as to draw blood, his hand shall be cut off; that if a pilgrim strike another with the palm of his hand or so that no blood be drawn, then he shall be plunged into the sea three times.[5]

Other concerns included the health risks posed to pregnant women undertaking arduous journeys, such as that to the Holy Land. In one account by Felix Fabri, he relates how a storm at sea left the pilgrims on board shaken and seasick. He creates a vivid picture of the condition on ship during this storm as well as the shortage of food and drink. A pregnant woman is among the party:

> When day broke, as the storm still continued, we remained quiet, and bore our lot with patience, as we were without food or drink, for there was no fire in the galley, and the kitchen on deck was full of water; besides which we were all sea-sick, and loathed all food and drink, because our stomachs were upset. Indeed, if anyone had eaten anything while that storm lasted he would not have kept it down, but would have vomited it up again. There is nothing better than to keep one's stomach empty during storms. Moreover, all our bread was spoilt and uneatable with salt water, and therefore we were compelled to fast.

On their arrival at the port of Lesina, Fabri relates how all were relieved to refresh themselves and clear their heads of their lingering seasickness. However, they also waited there for three days to enable the pregnant woman in their party to recover her strength, for she 'had suffered much and become very weak during the gale; indeed, it is a wonder that both she and her infant did not perish during that terrible time'.[6]

There is evidence that women did die while on pilgrimages. In one instance, an inquest is held but the heir is absent for she herself had died while in the Holy Land. The neighbours with whom she had travelled had returned safely and attested to her death. We do not know the exact circumstances of her death, but as such mischances as robbery, rape or kidnap of a pilgrim are often cited in such evidence, we may assume that hers was from natural causes.

Felix Fabri's accounts and advice for pilgrims to the Holy Land often give a clear idea of the many hazards they faced that could lead to their injury, sickness or even demise. Some of these hazards were simply part of the challenges the pilgrim had to overcome and were inherent in the pilgrimage experience – including perfecting the dangerous leap from the galley on arrival in Jaffa into the boat that would row them to shore, a leap that was often misjudged. It is noted as one of the more common hazards. Fabri explains that this leap is particularly treacherous in rough seas, when the constant rise and fall of the waves make it near impossible to disembark from the galley into the boat without either falling into the sea or landing badly in the boat. He remarks that in some cases, pilgrims preferred to forego the opportunity to step ashore for a while rather than brave the jump.

In such weather [one must] watch carefully until the boat comes so near to the galley that he can reach it by a leap, for the men will not allow the boat to come nearer than this; and he must leap the instant it comes so close, for unless he leaps, the next moment it is carried further away from the galley by the waves, and when he does leap into the boat he cannot save himself from falling, either forwards or backwards, on his face or his back, and those on board of it lift him up.[7]

Considering that few people were accustomed to water or indeed to swimming, it is perhaps no surprise that numbers of pilgrims were drowned. A papal letter of 11 May 1330 cites a pilgrim, Matilda de Brionie of London, who on her way to visit the Holy Land, Assisi and Santiago was in a boat that capsized in the Rhône leaving Valence. While many of her companions drowned, Matilda managed to survive, but she lost her provisions and money and so was forced to abandon her pilgrimage. Her story is documented in papal letters that concern her request to transmute her vow by entering a convent as she is now without the means to complete her pilgrimage.[8]

Records and anecdotes of women on pilgrimage consistently attest to the bravery and gregarious nature of many of their number in the face of great challenges or peril. One memorable experience was that of a tenth-century Icelandic pilgrim who embarked on several pilgrimage journeys with each of her three husbands. The intrepid Gudrid of Iceland[9] survived shipwreck and other adventures on her travels, giving birth to her son Snorri on the way possibly, as some accept, the first European to be born in North America. Gudrid is also known to have made a pilgrimage on foot to Rome in 1051. She ended her days in Iceland where she was credited with the foundation of several nunneries. While not the stereotypical European pilgrim with which we are perhaps more familiar, Gudrid broadens our knowledge of early medieval pilgrims as an intrepid female traveller who set out aboard Viking ships rather than the more conventional pilgrim galley. She embraced Christianity, ending her days as a nun and anchoress in a pattern common to several other women pilgrims and mystics both before and after her.

Of all the pilgrimage destinations, the Holy Land offered the newest and most unfamiliar experiences to the pilgrim. Those venturing to this, the holiest of destinations, needed to be aware of what lay in store if they were to enjoy a safe stay. Its inhabitants, the Muslim infidels, were considered unbelievers by Christians and they adhered to a totally alien set of religious practices, something that is frequently mentioned in the surviving accounts of pilgrims who witnessed at first hand their different social customs. After Jerusalem fell to the crusaders in 1099, most of them who did not return to their homelands became dedicated to establishing independent Christian states and protecting pilgrim routes to holy places. The protection of Latin pilgrims to the Holy Land by such orders of knights as the Templars received papal endorsement. At a council of the Church in 1124 at Troyes, France, the Knights Templar became established as an official military-religious order and protector of the pilgrim. From the fourteenth century, a Franciscan community based on Mount Sion also looked after the Latin pilgrims' safety, while pilgrims themselves could also rely on the advice of others as a means of remaining sensible to the dangers of their unfamiliar surroundings.

Contemporary pilgrim guide-books often cautioned as to what it was best to avoid doing in the Holy Land. Things were done differently there, as Brother Felix Fabri notes of his own two journeys. Quite sensibly, his advice often concerns the appeasing and indulging of their hosts' demands and sensibilities. On arrival at the port of Jaffa, pilgrims would continue their journey on land to Jerusalem by ass under the control of Saracen guides. Fabri points out that it is worth taking trouble to choose an ass that looks lively for if the pilgrim ends up with a slow beast, they would be left behind – and one pays just as much for a slow ass as for a faster one. Finally, the pilgrim should not try to exchange their ass in case such an act angered their host.

His advice is specific and prudent. For example, he cautions pilgrims against making a show of laughter or merriment in front of the Saracens lest the latter become suspicious and think themselves the butt of their jokes. Equally important, pilgrims should not offend the Saracens by wearing white turbans, or winding white cloths about their heads, as this was not their privilege. Other restrictions that Latin pilgrims did well to observe were to refrain from entering mosques or into their cities other than on foot. Fabri also noted that the Saracens were easily vexed by pilgrims who stepped over the tombs of their dead. Failure to respect these differences could lead to skirmishes and disillusionment between the two parties, which might end in the Latin pilgrims coming under attack. Consciousness of these differences in culture and sensibility made pilgrims acutely aware of the dangers they might face should they encounter opposition from the Saracens or, indeed, find themselves separated from their pilgrim party.

An account of pilgrims to the Holy Land who lose a female member of their party conjures up the potential dangers awaiting pilgrims in the Holy Land as the party entertain their worst fears as to what may have befallen her. She may have drowned in the River Jordan or be stuck fast in mud on its banks; she may have collapsed from hunger or exhaustion; she may have been seized, robbed or defiled by some Saracen, carried off by a local shepherd or even attacked and devoured by a lion or some other wild beast. After much wailing by her female companions and the despatch of a search party on horseback, she is found fast asleep but perfectly safe among a bed of reeds, having been bathing in the Jordan. 'They awakened her, took her up, placed her upon a horse, and came up to us with glad cries, as though they had taken a wild beast.'[10]

In this anecdote the reaction of the male members of the party to the woman having become separated from the group is also of interest. There is a definite air of disgruntlement among some 'rough and hard hearted knights' who resent the disruption caused by the delay. In an ironic twist, Fabri takes care to point out that the man who complained the loudest later found himself indebted to this woman, who nurses him when he is taken gravely ill: 'and with tears [he] begged for help from those whom he had scorned before'. It is, however, probable that had it not been for the presence of the woman's female companions, who by their hysterics and shrieks halt the party in its tracks or, indeed, perhaps for the presence of the kind-hearted Brother Fabri, such a woman might simply have been left behind.

We may recall that Margery Kempe experienced similar indifference from some of her male pilgrim companions. In the Holy Land, she struggles up the Mount of Temptation (Mount Sinai), thirsty and weary. Medieval accounts speak of the challenge that this journey posed for visiting pilgrims, one describing it simply as 'passyngly hote and ryght hyghe . . .'.[11] Her male companions continue without any regard for her until, as Kempe's account describes, an unexpected rescuer comes to her aid.[12]

The accounts of the fourth-century Spanish nun Egeria also testify to the physical endurance required by some of the climbs and hikes of the Holy Land tours; she talks of the many hills and climbs around Sinai before one reaches the summit of the Mount itself: 'You do not go round and round them, spiralling up gently, but straight at each one as if you were going up a wall, and then straight down to the foot, till you reach the foot of the central mountain, Sinai itself. Here then . . . we made the great effort of the climb . . .'[13]

Food and illness were ever-present challenges and concerns for pilgrims to the Holy Land. The recorded journeys of the fifteenth-century fellow of Eton, William Wey (1408–76), to Santiago de Compostela and twice to the Holy Land, offered the most candid advice for pilgrims. Wey's verse and prose were heavily drawn upon by William Caxton's successor, the printer Wynkyn de Worde, when he compiled his *Information for Pilgrims unto the Holy Land*: '. . . beware of fruytes that ye ete none for no thynge. As melons and suche colde fruytes, for they be not accordynge to our complexyon & they gendre a blody fluxe [diarrhoea]. And yf ony enghysshe man catche there that syknesse, it is a grete merueylle but yt he deye therof.'[14] And regarding food that was necessary for provisions: 'Also whan ye shall ryde to flume Jordan take wyth you out of Jerusalem brede, wyne, water, harde eggys and chese, and suche vytaylles as ye maye haue for two dayes. For by alle that waye there is none to selle.'[15]

Another very real hazard which is discussed in pilgrim accounts was overcrowding. In the twelfth century, Abbot Suger had embarked on an ambitious building project at St Denis Abbey, home to a number of important holy relics. His reasons for this expansion related to the vast numbers of pilgrims coming to visit the relics and the limited amount of space available:

> Often . . . the excess of the crowds as they moved in opposite directions, and the outward pressure of the foremost ones not only prevented those attempting to enter from entering, but also expelled those who had already entered. The distress of the women, however, was so great . . . that you could see with horror how they, squeezed in by the mass of strong men as in a winepress, exhibited bloodless faces as in imagined death.[16]

Indeed, most of those crushed at the St Denis of Abbot Suger's time were women who had gathered in enthusiastic anticipation of seeing the relics. In the moment of a bottle-neck crush in the narrowest parts of the church, those women who were able were seen to run to the altar over the heads and shoulders of other male pilgrims in their anguish. Accounts of overcrowding at other reliquary sites also tell of pregnant women being crushed to death in the throng that had gathered to see the head of St Martial.[17]

The holy sites in Jerusalem were also on occasion besieged by tides of pilgrims which resulted in a dangerous compress in the enclosed spaces of the Church of the Holy Sepulchre. Theoderich's accounts show that such overcrowding continued well into the thirteenth century when the Sepulchre's wardens devised ways to avert disaster. He describes the sheer weight of pilgrim traffic that vied for space within the chapel of Mount Calvary alone: 'Here, at the top of the stairs, stand Guardians watching the gate, who only allow as many pilgrims as they choose to enter, lest by excessive pressure, as often happens, there is crushing or danger to life.'[18]

Rome became particularly prone to overcrowding especially with the introduction of its Jubilee years, celebrations initiated by Pope Boniface VIII. The first was held in 1300 and attracted a huge number of pilgrims on account of the plenary indulgence promised to all those visiting the basilicas of Sts Peter and Paul. Originally announced as a centenary celebration, Clement VI eventually sanctioned its celebration every fifty years, so that the next Jubilee was set for 1350. Such Jubilees excited the interest of large numbers of pilgrims who descended on Rome and the pilgrimage circuit of prescribed basilicas in order to benefit from the indulgence. The chronicler Villani attested to the great number of pilgrims in Rome in the first Jubilee year of 1300:

> And it was the most remarkable thing that ever was seen, that during the whole year there were in Rome, besides the Roman people, 200,000 pilgrims, not counting those who were coming and going along the roads . . . and I can bear witness, for I was there and I saw. . . . And from the offerings made to the church and to the Romans; all were made rich by their takings. . . .[19]

One chronicle for 1300 relates how, on Christmas Eve, the number of pilgrims leaving Rome was so great that it was said there must be 'twenty hundred thousand men and women there': 'Several times I saw both men and women trampled under the feet of others and on several occasions I myself escaped the same danger.'[20] By 1350, similar crowds were seen to arrive in Rome again for the Jubilee, each man and woman now also required to visit the basilica of St John in Laterano, as well as those of Sts Peter and Paul in order to receive their indulgence. Here pilgrims would have the chance to see those holy relics pertaining to the birth and circumcision of the Lord. Chroniclers noted the slow-moving crowds of pilgrims in the streets, progressing from one basilica to the next, as well as the overcrowding of the inns at night with Romans becoming self-appointed innkeepers in order to accommodate all the pilgrims. With demand outstripping supply, some shop-keepers, grocers and butchers were also accused of making excessive profits.

New to the 1350 Jubilee was the public display of the *sudarium* of Veronica, the cloth or veil said to have been handed to Christ by a holy matron of Jerusalem, Veronica, who accompanied Him to Calvary. The veil was said to have been left with the impression of Christ's face and thus naturally assumed the status of a highly valuable relic. The *sudarium* was exhibited in public every Sunday afternoon at St Peter's and the chance to gaze upon the counten-ance of Christ would have been an opportunity taken by many pilgrims to Rome. It seems also that its popularity may have supplanted that of the holy relics of St Peter themselves. However, in their eagerness to see the relics even greater numbers of pilgrims were trampled and crushed.

Wealthy pilgrims might successfully apply for a private viewing of the *sudarium*, but for the majority it was a case of battling the crowd, risking suffocation and the possibility of being trampled underfoot. A chronicle of the events of the Jubilee by Heinrich von Rebdorff recounted how he witnessed several pilgrims crushed to death in such crowds gathered to view Veronica's *sudarium*. Smaller, frailer or indeed pregnant women might find themselves in the greatest peril in such episodes. John Capgrave highlights this danger when he discusses the enthusiasm of women pilgrims to see and touch all the holy relics on offer in Rome; he states that the areas in which such holy relics were displayed were often 'rit smale. . . . And uphap some women in the press, either for sikness or with child, be in grete perel there . . .'. He even cites such a scenario as a reason for forbidding entry to women at such popular shrines.[21]

St Bridget of Sweden's writings alert us to a different sort of peril of which pilgrims to Rome for the 1350 Jubilee would have been aware, in the shape of a natural disaster that occurred shortly beforehand. She describes the effects of an earthquake on Rome, where many of the holy buildings exhibited cracks and pieces of fallen masonry. Roofs were unsteady and 'mosaic floors, once fresh and beautiful, were now broken in pieces and the faithful stumbled into holes in the floor, doing themselves great injury'.

Perhaps the worst and best-documented tragedy to affect pilgrims to Rome was the collapse of the bridge of Ponte Sant Angelo in the year of the 1450 Jubilee. It occurred on Saturday 19 December after pilgrims had gathered to view the *sudarium*, had received their indulgences and were on their way back. One account states that a mule carrying two women and a small load took fright on the bridge because of the oppressive crowd trying to cross. This in turn sent a wave of pilgrims tumbling across the bridge under whose weight the bridge collapsed. The account states that 200 people and 3 horses drowned as a result and many more fell into the river or were injured. 'Some of the dead were taken to Santo Cello and part to the Campo Santo, where eighteen cartloads full of dead people were carried. Never was such a thing seen or heard of, such a horrible event.'[22]

Other less life-threatening but nevertheless discomforting aspects of medieval pilgrimage might include hygiene, or that of your companions. There was no guarantee of standards of hospitality en route and the conditions on board a pilgrim galley could be particularly unsanitary, with vermin nibbling away at food supplies, bedding and clothes and any other bugs carried by pilgrims quickly spreading to all. Every Christian was encouraged to shelter and feed travelling pilgrims and thereby reap some of the virtue of their holy journey. The rich might be in a better position to avoid vermin-infested inns or taverns, perhaps by sending ahead one of their retinue to assess a particular inn. In one case, the servant returns with reassurances of the hospitality offered by the tavern, 'no sir . . . for please God you will be well and comfortably lodged there – except that we suffer much from rats and mice'.

While most pilgrims would be used to fleas and vermin in their own home environment, Margery Kempe's experience reveals how the mixing of different classes of pilgrim could make such conditions a common problem. She falls in with a company of poorer, flea-ridden pilgrims who were surviving their journey on charity and by begging. Having witnessed their frequent disrobing in order to pick themselves free of vermin, she discovers that it is not just their company that she has shared: 'she caught some of their vermin and was dreadfully bitten and stung both day and night, until God sent her other companions'.[23]

Pilgrims might even find themselves unwittingly caught up in political unrest, such as those who happened to be on the trail from Canterbury back to London on the day of the Peasants' Revolt, 11 June 1381. The pilgrims were held up by the rebels and forced to swear their allegiance to King Richard and their rejection of John, Duke of Lancaster, as well as being coerced into committing themselves to their cause, vowing to make themselves available when called upon and to spread the rebels' message among their own village folk concerning the rejection of new taxes! Perhaps most significantly, King Richard's own mother, Joan of Kent, also chanced to be returning from the shrine of Becket in Canterbury that day and was caught up in the fray of rebels bound on their defiant protest to London:

> there returned from Kent the King's mother . . . coming from her pilgrimage. . . . She was in great jeopardy to have been lost, for these people came to her chare and dealt rudely with her, whereof the good lady was in great doubt lest they would have done some villainy to her or to her damosels. Howbeit, God kept her, and she came in one day from Canterbury to London, for she durst tarry by the way. . . .[24]

ELEVEN

Dreams, Miracles and Hysteria – Women as Supplicants and Devotees

[W]e came to the spot where the Lord, while bearing His cross, hearing and seeing pitiful outcries of women who were following Him, turned away . . . from the raging mob to the women who loved Him, and were mourning for Him, saying, 'Ye daughters of Jerusalem, weep not for Me.'[1]

As we have seen, medieval women were generally considered to be less stable of temperament than their male counterparts and, in consequence, more prone to emotional or imaginative excess. Some of the surviving accounts of women on pilgrimage and at shrines are so emotionally charged and ecstatic as to seem almost hallucinatory, to take Margery Kempe and St Paula as among the most obvious examples. One might fairly argue that such female behaviour is rooted in history and the wailing and weeping of women are often described in the Bible.

Female saints themselves are interesting precursors to such theatrical expressions of piety, which might also include episodes of self-deprivation. St Catherine of Siena was recorded as eating nothing for several years except for the communion host. Her tutor, Raymond of Capua, wrote a life of his pupil and noted her death at thirty-three years old. Another popular woman saint, Etheldreda (d. 679), had been married two times but apparently remained a virgin throughout. She left her second husband when he demanded sexual relations with her, instead entering the religious life as an abbess. With money and property most likely acquired through her dowry and marriages, she founded a monastery.

The accounts of both Margery Kempe and St Bridget show each to have been almost utterly overcome at holy shrines, seemingly reliving the emotions and physical experience of the historic event on a very personal level, a phenomenon most clearly apparent in Kempe's experience of the Holy Land sites. Here, pilgrims were able to see for themselves numerous places intimately connected with the life and times of Christ and the holy family. These holy locations of Christ's life, suffering and death were marked out for pilgrim visitors who could stand in awe in the place where Jesus was buried, where He was nailed to the cross and where He was crucified. Every aspect of the sites' arrangement encouraged visitors to relive and re-create Jesus's life and the events leading up to and including his death and burial, while the emotions and grief of the original protagonists could be re-enacted by pilgrims such as Margery Kempe and, indeed, many women before her.

When this creature and her companions came to the grave where our Lord was buried, then, as she entered that holy place, she fell down with her candle in her hand, as if she would have died for sorrow.[2]

Holy shrines would have been highly charged with an emotional and anticipatory atmosphere to which both male and female pilgrims would have been subject. In his accounts of his second trip to the Holy Land, Brother Fabri of Ulm describes in some detail the reaction of pilgrims on arrival at the Holy Sepulchre: they prostrate themselves, kissing the ground as if, he says, they believe that the very ground might transmute some of the holy energy of the place. Of particular note are the emotional displays of the women:

Above all our companions and sisters the women pilgrims shrieked as though in labour, cried aloud and wept. Some pilgrims, out of excess of devotion, lost all command of themselves, forgot how they should behave, and out of excessive zeal to please God, made strange and childish gestures.[3]

The implication seems to be that these women were articulating their affective piety as a very public performance, to be interpreted as a conspicuous measure of the depth of their piety and 'to please God'. Such emotional episodes could also be part of a larger experience for the pilgrim that was intensely physical as well as mental and must have involved a degree of anxiety in the face of their expectations. By the late Middle Ages some also believed that simply by entering a holy place, the suppliant could be spiritually cleansed and renewed so that all past sins were absolved; this was a significant factor for the pilgrim who hoped to transmute some of his or her suffering in Purgatory into arduous pilgrimage. Again, such beliefs find their precursors in early writings and narrative episodes, such as that of the Swedish mystic St Bridget purportedly told by Christ in a vision that she would be cleansed of all her sins the moment she entered the basilica of the Holy Sepulchre as if after a baptism. This experience in itself might constitute a kind of psychological rebirthing for some pilgrims, so that the spiritual intensity of the moment was heightened even before they laid eyes on the holy relics. In keeping with this notion, pilgrims to the Holy

Land also ritually bathed in the River Jordan in a conscious re-
enactment of the Baptism:

> Too mile fro the Ded See
> In Jordan Pylgremys whasched be . . .[4]

For some, this process might also bring about a miraculous cure,
'Naaman of Syria bathed himself in that river [Jordan] seven times,
and he was healed of his leprosy and made sound as a fish. . . .'[5]

There was also a river close to Santiago de Compostela near the
end of their journey, where pilgrims would wash themselves in
preparation for entry into the hallowed space of St James's
Cathedral. Aimery Picaud, a twelfth-century French cleric from
Parthenay Le Vieux, was the author of a five-volume pilgrims' guide
to the routes to Santiago de Compostela. Picaud wrote that the
practice of bathing in the river before entering the city was an act of
reverence to the apostle saint, but for some hapless pilgrims it also
meant losing their clothing to thieves. Such episodes of ritual
bathing or spiritual cleansing prior to and on entering a holy place
served as a catalyst, intensifying the emotional experience
for pilgrims.

In the case of Margery Kempe, such heightened emotion coupled
with her strong sense of attachment to the holy places she visits
prompted great outpourings of emotion, so that it is as if she were
visiting the grave of one of her own family. The experience of loss,
bereavement and suffering appears to have been very real for
women pilgrims such as Kempe, often accompanied not only by
dramatic emotional displays but also subsequently engendering a
greater volatility, fertile ground for the reporting of visions. At the
Holy Sepulchre, Kempe believes she can almost see Jesus's corpse
laid out before her, enhanced by a powerful visual evocation of His
weeping mother, bereft and lamenting the loss of her Son. It is a
subconscious evocation of the pietà scene that is extensively
illustrated in art, in illumination manuscripts, on rood screens, in

stained glass and other imagery with which Kempe and women pilgrims like her would have been familiar. Mary Magdalene was also frequently portrayed in art as the penitent, weeping woman, her name and behaviour most likely giving rise to the modern use of the word 'maudlin' to mean over-sentimental, weepy or mawkish.

Such visions and apparitions could sometimes be very dramatic and accompanied by various other physical responses. In the case of the twelfth-century mystic, theologian and composer Hildegard of Bingen, the sceptic might compare her symptoms to those that can accompany migraines, including flashes of light and distortions of peripheral vision. Subsequently, Hildegard has been dubbed by some as the most distinguished migraine sufferer. It is not the aim of this study to attempt either to authenticate or disprove such accounts and, as with the countless miracle cures reported by male and female pilgrims alike, this would be a near impossible task. For our purposes, though, the reported experience of visions, hysteria and even hysterics was clearly more predominant among female pilgrims than male and a significant component of the medieval woman's pilgrimage experience. Given that pilgrims might also be viewing such sensational items as bleeding images of Christ or those of the Virgin that apparently shed real tears, it would seem that the drama surrounding some pilgrimage shrines and reliquary displays demanded equally affective responses from their audience, who strove to demonstrate their heartfelt appreciation and pious involvement.

It might be argued that women with their mothering tendencies could more readily make an emotional connection with the events of the Lord's Passion and the Virgin's loss and that the earthly backdrop for these events created the perfect conditions for such heightened emotional awareness and empathy. Interestingly, these sorts of reactions, are far less frequently reported for male pilgrims visiting such sites. The theatre of emotional display seems to be a stage predominantly reserved for the female pilgrim, but one that could also be to her detriment, such as in the case of Margery Kempe.

Kempe's dictated account of her pilgrimages includes several references to her 'loud cryings at the memory of Our Lord's Passion', 'violent sobbings' and 'abundant tears of compassion', much to the annoyance of the rest of her party:

And they were most annoyed because she wept so much and spoke all the time about the love and goodness of our Lord . . . and said they would not put up with her as her husband did when she was at home in England.[6]

As a result, her relations with her pilgrim companions also get off to a rocky start during their six-week delay at Bristol.[7] During this time, she attends communion every Sunday and indulges in her customary displays of 'plentiful tears and violent sobbings with loud crying and shrill shriekings', much to the fury of the rest of the congregation. Her emotional eruptions incite vitriolic insults and threats so that even before she has boarded ship, she has made an adequate number of enemies. Only a small number perceive her behaviour as an admirable if public articulation of genuine devotion.

Before embarkation, Kempe prays for her own protection and a safe return for all her companions, 'For she had been told that, if they had any storm, they would throw her into the sea, for they said it would be because of her; and they said the ship was the worse for her being in it.'[8] Not until their safe arrival at Santiago de Compostela do tensions ease, 'and those who were against her when they were in Bristol were now very nice to her'.

Emotional attachment to venerated sites was mirrored in that to holy relics, the articles alleged to have belonged to certain religious figures, saints and martyrs and of which those connected to the holy family were the most prized. The holy relic could consist of anything from bones and human remains to a fragment of cloth or any other item closely associated with the figure concerned. These objects were venerated as vestiges of the holy dead and supernatural powers were often attributed to them, namely the ability to perform miracles and to cure the sick and, in some cases, the power to withstand the natural processes of decomposition.[9]

'All those which be at Rome knowe well that the women there be passing desirous to goo on pilgrimage and to touch and kiss every holy relik. . . .'[10] Such relics came to be the mainstay and financial resource for many a religious centre with pilgrims flocking to bear witness to them, many in hope of divine dispensation or a miracle cure. Geary's study of the popularity and theft of holy relics highlights their significance for the medieval pilgrim as 'the point of contact between mundane existence and the divine world. They were part of the sacred, the numinous; but incarnated in this world, as had been Christ, without losing their place in the other.'[11]

Those relics associated with Jesus and the holy family such as fragments of the True Cross, the crown of thorns, nails, even drops of the holy blood were highly prized by their keepers and much esteemed by pilgrims. The church of St Chapelle in France boasted impressively of ownership of the crown of thorns, fragments of the purple cloak of Christ, as well as pieces of the True Cross, while the cathedral of Chartres in northern France was one of several that claimed ownership of the tunic of the Virgin Mary. Equally, any articles that could be carried away from a holy site such as souvenirs and lead ampullae of holy water were treated as a form of portable relic that could be taken back home and its powers invoked in much the same way for miracle cures or divine intervention. Such items often carried the stamp of the religious centre concerned and pictured its affiliated saint. It was also believed that by placing such items in the vicinity of the holy relics themselves, some of the supernatural or spiritual potency of the deceased figure could be transmuted to the objects concerned:

Should he wish to bring back a relic from the tomb, he carefully weighs a piece of cloth which he then hangs inside the tomb. Then he prays ardently and, if his faith is sufficient, the cloth, once removed from the tomb, will be found to be so full of divine grace that it will be much heavier than before. Thus will he know that his prayers have been granted.[12]

Pilgrims were thus attracted by the opportunity to harness some of the perceived supernatural energy of their chosen saint in this tangible form. Women have been depicted as particularly ardent collectors of such objects for the purpose of aiding the cure of loved ones. In the satirical description of a husband and wife at the shrine of Le Puy in France, we saw how the husband is pushed to the middle of the crowd by his wife in order to touch the holy relic with her girdle, only to be sent back on a souvenir-hunting mission wherein he is crushed and trodden on for his efforts.[13]

Perhaps one of the most intriguing narratives describing women's emotional attachment to such objects, as well as the spiritual power associated with relics appears, unsurprisingly, in Margery Kempe's account. She describes a woman whom she encounters who carries with her a chest inside of which is an image of Christ. On arrival at a city, the woman would place the chest in the laps of 'respectable wives. . . . And they would dress it up in shirts and kiss it as though it had been God himself . . .'. The gesture of placing the holy image in the woman's lap to rest against her womb is significant, reinforcing the association with childbearing and fertility. Its potency and symbolism would have been acknowledged and understood by those concerned. As for Margery Kempe, she is as demonstrative as ever, 'she was so much the more moved because, while she was in England, she had high meditations on the birth and childhood of Christ . . .'.[14]

There are some parallels here with the legend of St Veronica. She is believed to have offered Christ her veil (or *sudarium*) on which was left the imprint of His face. This cloth was taken to Rome and became a highly venerated article on public display. It is thought that the name Veronica was derived from the Latin *vera icon*, or true image or likeness. That pilgrims could worship the image of Christ was a powerful concept that would have ranked closely with

162

the opportunity to walk the ground that Jesus had trodden in the Holy Land.

Another response to the personal experience of relics and holy sites was the tradition of the woman being subject to dreams, visions and visitations. While such experiences were not the exclusive domain of women, female pilgrims are the subject of some of the most dramatic accounts. For example, in 1061 a Saxon noblewoman from Norfolk, Richeldis de Faverches, claimed to have received a visitation from the Virgin Mary in her sleep. Again, such episodes had their parallel in much earlier, biblical accounts of the Anunciation and Visitation. In this instance, Richeldis, a wealthy widow, claimed that the Virgin visited her in a dream in order to instruct her on the building of a new religious house in Norfolk. She was taken on a virtual journey to the house in Nazareth where the Anunciation had taken place, the home in which Jesus had lived and been brought up. Richeldis claims that she was prompted by the Virgin to make a mental note of all that she saw, including the building's dimensions, in order that she could build an exact replica of the house back in Walsingham, Norfolk. Once the holy house was complete, it was to be sanctioned by the Virgin who had prompted its creation. Of course, there was also the prestige associated with the idea of the mother of Christ having handpicked the then tiny backwater of Walsingham as the resting place for her Nazarean home. These events saw the beginning of Walsingham as an esteemed destination on the pilgrim itinerary, particularly popular with women on account of its cult of the Virgin and the story behind its foundation. From 1061 it came to be revered as 'England's Nazareth'.

If the building of a new holy house based on the isolated reverie of a widow constituted proof that such dreams were accepted as divine messages, then there is much other evidence to corroborate this type of popular acceptance. In the eleventh century a woman with crippled hands requested to be allowed to touch the body of St Gilles in Provence. Most often, only proxy contact was permitted with the pilgrim where holy relics were concerned, through the medium of holy water, dust or objects that had been brought into physical contact with them. In this case the female pilgrim uses a dream she had had the previous night in support of her request, arguing that in it she had been told she would be cured if only she could touch the relics. It is the extenuating circumstance of her dream that sees her request granted.

Women brought the highly charged devotional energy often attributed to them to shrines such as Walsingham, which saw an unprecedented rise to fame. There is some evidence to suggest that the advantages of women pilgrims' involvement in increasing a shrine's popularity did not go unnoticed. At the shrine of St Edmund of Canterbury at Pontigny a new crucifix had been made for the lay-brothers' choir. When it was found to be capable of performing miracles, the mutual benefits of allowing women access to the crucifix were immediately recognised: 'Wherefore it was thought that if women could have access to the crucifix, the general fervour would be increased and our monastery would derive no little benefit from it. . . .'[15] As elsewhere, presumably the intention was that women pilgrims would benefit the monastery not just through their fervent devotions at the shrine, but also by word-of-mouth recommendation of the shrine and its miracles, so encouraging further visitors and women devotees.

While the well-documented tearful displays, even hysteria, of women are sometimes explained by an already volatile disposition, one must also consider why it was that women more commonly than men were the protagonists in such ethereal experiences as auspicious dreams, visions and ecstasies. As mentioned earlier, men were not exempt from these experiences and indeed it was a visitation by Sts Peter and Paul to a monk at the Abbey of Cluny that was said to have inspired the commencement of a third stage of building there. However, such incidents are apparently more common or at least more extensively documented for women. It has been argued that men were perhaps more sceptical as the subject of such experiences, while women were more receptive to the possibility of such occurrences so that in the event, there could also be a difference in interpretation between men and women as to their meaning and cause. Perhaps women were more inclined to share such experiences with others, so spreading the concept and possibility of such events among other women. Analysis of this topic and the surviving evidence for it demands its own study, but it is important here to highlight some of those experiences and the women subjects concerned.

Certainly, women's experiences of such events do not appear to have been ignored and again we may look to biblical accounts of the events that may well have acted as subconscious endorsement for the medieval psyche. The Virgin, a cult figure in the Middle Ages, was the subject of many such episodes including the Visitation, Annunciation and the divine conception of the Christ child. It was Mary Magdalene who, in the company of two other women, set out to anoint the corpse of Christ, revealing the fact that his body had miraculously vanished from the place where it had lain, and it is Mary and Martha, the sisters of Lazarus, who play major roles in the events of the raising of his body. The Bible speaks of many more such highly symbolic events, all of which would have been familiar to a medieval audience through oral teachings or depiction in murals and other visual arts.

In narrative and biblical terms, therefore, auspicious dreams, ecstasies and visions were usually the domain of saints, martyrs and holy figures. It seems likely, however, that some of the more austerely religious or female mystics, anchoresses and the like would have aspired to emulate such venerated figures in their own behaviour and experience. Certainly Margery Kempe appears to have found the model for some of her behaviour in her beloved St Bridget, famed for her own hysterical outpourings, as well as in the fourteenth-century mystic and anchorite Mother Julian of Norwich who professes her own better understanding of her spirituality to be facilitated through 'actual vision, in imaginative understanding, and in spiritual sight'.[16] Other such predecessors include Paula who left

Rome to reside in Bethlehem. In his letters, her fellow resident and friend St Jerome who compiled his translation of the Bible there, waxes lyrical about Paula and her ascetically stalwart spirit. He describes her emotional response the first time she visited the holy places which has a familiar ring:

> After this she came to Bethlehem and entered the cave where the Saviour was born; and when she looked upon the inn, the stall and the crib . . . she cried out in my hearing that with the eyes of her soul she could see the infant Christ wrapped in swaddling clothes and crying in the manger.[17]

Kempe continually exhibits her own saintly aspirations through her emotional responses as well as the way of life she chooses on pilgrimage. One might also say that in this way, whether consciously or subconsciously, some women were able to assert their position in a society that held them to be inferior.

In his study, Ronald C. Finucane shows that women constituted a significant number of those pilgrims reporting miraculous cures and life-saving interventions at holy shrines. This evidence often relates to the high proportion of children who had been accidentally injured, drowned, stillborn and so on, protagonists in miracle testimonials, thus directly highlighting women and mothers as beneficiaries of miraculous intervention.[18]

The stained-glass windows in Canterbury Cathedral[19] are a wonderful example of illustrated miracle cycles involving women as the recipients of divine cures. A nun, Petronella of Polesworth, appears at the shrine of Becket apparently suffering from epilepsy. She is assisted by other nuns to the tomb where her cure is administered through the bathing of her feet in the holy water of St Thomas. The ampullae that contained such holy water for carrying away from the shrine often bore the assertion of St Thomas's mastery as *optimus egrorum: medicus fit toma bonorum*, 'the best doctor of the worthy sick'.

In another window, Ethelreda of Canterbury receives a cure for her condition through imbibing the blood of St Thomas, and the two daughters of Godbald of Boxley, both lame from birth, are cured when St Thomas appears to them in dreams. Juliana of Rochester is depicted with her eyes sealed shut in blindness being led to St Thomas's tomb by her father. The application of the blood of St Thomas to her eyes brings about her eventual cure, for which Juliana and her father are seen to give thanks back at their home.

Another dramatically rendered scene concerns a young child, Geoffrey of Winchester. Having already had his rescue from a fever as a baby attributed to the curative powers of St Thomas, his mother calls on the saint a second time when her house collapses and her son is trapped inside. She implores St Thomas to save the life of the boy he had already once returned to her. In a central scene, she is represented amid the pandemonium of her collapsed home, fainting while men search through the rubble; then, in a final scene, she is shown leaning over her son, who has been found safe among the debris.

A woman from Cologne is another beneficiary of a cure depicted in the Canterbury windows, this time from a madness. Depicted wide-eyed and in a bacchanalian-like stance with wild hair and gesticulating hands, she had apparently killed her infant child in a fit of rage on discovering that her brother had killed her lover. The stained glass portrays her being beaten with sticks and left bound at Becket's tomb. Her recovery begins with a vision in which St Thomas tells her to go on another pilgrimage to Santiago de Compostela and there receive absolution for her sins. In a final scene she is shown in a more composed state, kneeling in supplication at the tomb while her companions relinquish their beating sticks as votive offerings at the shrine.

Other miracles reported to have occurred at Becket's shrine were recorded by two monks, William and Benedict. A great number of these relate to symptoms of digestive disorders, for example abdominal pain, constipation and food poisoning. Interestingly, in his own account of Becket's miracles, Benedict of Peterborough noted that the effects of overeating and drinking were to be considered possible and preventable causes of discomfort by pregnant or breastfeeding women attending Becket's shrine.

All the above represent the deeper psychological and ethereal connection that could be experienced at shrines, with many such instances being reported by women. Perhaps the intensity of women's behaviour and spiritual affinity with the Bible's holy places was to some extent expected by their contemporaries as a specifically feminine, outward expression of their inner piety and asceticism; even Margery Kempe's alarming displays were sometimes credited to the workings of the Holy Spirit. The emotional displays, visions, hysteria and visitations of women pilgrims opens many avenues for psychological examination. As well as providing an invaluable insight into their mindset, such an understanding is essential for a complete assessment of the medieval woman's experience of pilgrimage.

TWELVE

Pilgrimage under Fire – Controversy and Decline

The surest thing for the soul's profit and the body's honour is to avoid the habit of trotting here and there.[1]

Much of the most vociferous criticism of pilgrimage and its practice by women dates from the thirteenth to fifteenth centuries, but concerns about the safety of women on such journeys had been expressed as early as the fourth century, when women are first documented as embarking on pilgrimage.

Commonly, women were accused of endangering their honour and modesty through pilgrimage and, in more extreme cases, of behaving with impropriety, lasciviousness and singing 'wanton songs'. Critics argued that a woman's place was in the home and others still that pilgrimage was being used as an excuse by women for a spring jaunt and a chance to escape their domestic responsibilities (a criticism that also came to be levelled at male pilgrims). Equally, there was concern that men and women pilgrims alike were embarking on aimless wanderings under the auspices of pilgrimage, their travels sometimes transmuted into life-long drifting and lacking any religious purpose.

One such critic was the thirteenth-century Franciscan preacher Berthold of Regensburg, who argued against women pilgrims on the conventionally accepted grounds of domestic and familial duties. He stated that too often, the funds for such a journey were found at the expense of the family and children left behind. A view that Christine de Pisan in her handbook of manners for noblewomen seems to corroborate. She counselled that the good wife ought to 'stay at home gladly and not go every day traipsing hither and yon gossiping with the neighbours and visiting her chums to find out what everyone is doing. . . . Nor should she go off on these pilgrimages got up for no good reason and involving a lot of needless expense.'[2]

However, she advises that it is perfectly acceptable for noble ladies to wish to go on pilgrimage to holy shrines, as long as they do so with a devotional and contrite heart. This advice alludes to those women pilgrims of less virtuous reputation who undertook their journeys for reasons other than spiritual edification, as a social outing, sometimes behaving inappropriately along the way. More directly, she continues:

> Some women travel on pilgrimages away from town in order to frolic and kick up their heels in jolly company. But this is only sin and folly. It is a sin to use God as an excuse and shelter for frivolity. Such pilgrimages are entirely without merit. Nor should a young woman go trotting about town, as is the custom – on Monday to St Avoye; on Tuesday, to who knows where; on Friday to St Catherine; and elsewhere on other days . . . the surest thing for the soul's profit and the body's honour is to avoid the habit of trotting here and there.'[3]

De Pisan's rhetoric denounces the unchecked behaviour of some women that so dismayed their critics, upsetting the proper order of society by travelling together on the pretext of visiting holy shrines, a different one each day, but without any of the requisite spiritual intent that would validate a sacred journey. Concern at women gadding about is also played out in the literary figure of Chaucer's Wife of Bath, of whom he asserts with sardonic flattery, 'She koude muchel of wandrynge by the weye' (General Prologue, l. 467). Chaucer's Wife of Bath embodies the traits of the women satirised in misogynist literature, as well as those criticised in assessments of the state of pilgrimage in the fourteenth century.

In his General Prologue, Chaucer names as a common incentive for pilgrimage the opportunity to 'seken straunge strondes' (shores) and to enjoy 'felawshipe',[4] a reiteration of the contemporary sentiment voiced by Thomas a Kempis, who stated that 'men are often moved by curiosity and the urge for sight seeing, and one seldom hears that any amendment of life results'.[5] This was the argument employed against 'wandrynge' women 'traipsing hither and yon' at the risk of their honour and personal safety, as Christine de Pisan highlighted and others would assert as reasons against noble women of good repute as well as young women of little worldly experience setting out on pilgrimage.

Written for the benefit of his three motherless daughters, *The Booke of Thenseygementes and Techynge the Towre Made to His Doughters* was originally compiled by Geoffrey de la Tour-Landry in the fourteenth century and later printed by William Caxton in 1484. Geoffrey also wrote a moral guide for his sons, but that is sadly lost to us. At the time of writing, in about 1371, he had resolved to protect the interests of his children, firstly through teaching his daughters to read so that they might be wise to the dangers of the world, as well as stipulating several regulations that would restrict their freedom of movement and speech. His teachings were intended to guide, regulate and protect young women in matters ranging from travel to fasting, from the wearing of make-up to premarital sex, to gossiping. Included is his counsel against pilgrimage. In what is intended as an edifying moral lesson, he tells the story of a woman who undertakes pilgrimage as a cover for a tryst with her lover. They set out happily to a shrine of Our Lady, but while chatting together during mass, the woman is suddenly struck down with a paralysis so severe that it was impossible to tell whether she was alive or dead. The didactic thrust of the tale has the paralysed woman visited in visions by her parents and the Virgin, all of whom emphasise to her the significance of staying loyal to her husband. Restored to health, the woman duly lives out the rest of her days as a faithful wife and daughter on the basis of her profound experience.[6]

La Tour-Landry himself alludes to the undertaking of pilgrimage by many people as a means of personal gratification rather than out of any devotion of heart, and ends his moralising: 'And therfor here is an exaumple that nobody shulde go in holy pilgrimages for to fulfell no foly, plesaunce, nor the worlde, nor flesshely delite. But thei shulde go enterly with herte to serue God.'[7] One cannot help but wonder that the worthy Knight did not have the preservation of his family's reputation and honour in mind as well, given the harsh criticism directed at women who misused the purpose of pilgrimage. He therefore offers his own vehement counsel to his daughters. In another of his didactic tales, in a manner reminiscent of pilgrimage's harshest critics he states, 'the world is al tourned vpso doune, for worship is not kepte in her ryght regle, ne in her ryght estate, as it was wonte to be', people revelling instead in the 'delytes and folysshe plesaunces of this world . . .'.

The Knight's teachings expose the moral failings of many other women who too readily lend themselves to profane and carnal pleasures, as well as detailing the very public, humiliating and sometimes violent punishment meted out to them – an adulterous woman has her nose cut off by her husband and is otherwise disfigured in order to limit her chances of a profitable marriage.

Geoffrey de La Tour-Landry's counsel on pilgrimage for his daughters is very similar to that prescribed in another work of the time, 'The Fifteen Joys of Marriage' (discussed in Chapter 3), which also details the abuse of pilgrimage by a young girl for the purpose of profane love.

> All thei that gone on pilgrimage to a place for foule plesaunce more thane devocion of the place that thei go to, and coverithe thaire goinge with service of God, fowlithe and scornithe God and oure lady.[8]

The woman is cured and reformed so that when some months later her former lover comes to visit, he is amazed at her transformation, as well as being told in no uncertain terms that she will now love no man other than her husband.

'The Fifteen Joys of Marriage' cites many other women who use pilgrimage as a means of entertainment and sexual gratification, a chance to meet their lovers, rid themselves of their husbands or to trap men into marriage having become pregnant by someone else, and similar unworthy reasons.

By the close of the fifteenth century, the Church appeared to be losing some of its grip on society, albeit for some it was felt that the social and moral structures were much in need of attention. In his complaints against lack of faith and the public's weakening of pious discipline, the Dominican monk Brother Felix Fabri had noted that many necessary qualities were absent in his contemporaries, such as honesty in a merchant, honour from youths and among the female sex specifically, 'chastity from maidens, lowliness from widows, love from wedded folk, modesty from women . . .'.[9]

Given the climate at the time and apparent slippage of moral and spiritual values regarding pilgrimage, the concerns about such dangers for women who ventured from home came sharply into focus. Hence, they had more to prove than men in the way of virtue, honour and pious motive in order to gain consent for pilgrimage. In his letter of 1243 to Eleanor of Provence, England's queen and wife to Henry III (1216–72), Pope Innocent IV granted her permission to go on pilgrimage to the churches of Rome, bringing with her a retinue of ten 'good and honest' women. It is an unfortunate truth that for all the impropriety, violence and immoderation that occurred among medieval pilgrims, women were singled out for the harshest scrutiny.

Among fifteenth-century critics of pilgrimage were Lollard preachers such as William Thorpe:

> I know well that when divers men and women will go thus after their own wills, and finding out one pilgrimage they will ordain beforehand to have with them both men and women that can well sing wanton songs. And some other pilgrims will have them bagpipes so that every town that they come through shall know of their coming, what with the noise of their singing and the sound of their piping, what with the jangling of their Canterbury bells, and the barking out of dogs after them. They make more noise than if the King came there away with all his clarions and many other minstrels.[10]

Thorpe's critique again encapsulates concerns at the lack of proper devotional incentive among many undertaking pilgrimage. The fourteenth-century provincial cleric and author of the spiritual allegory *Piers the Ploughman* shared his view, highlighting the practice of pilgrimage as more of a social convention:

> And I saw pilgrims and palmers banding together to visit the shrines at Rome and Compostella. They went on with their way full of clever talk, and took leave to tell fibs about it for the rest of their lives. And some I heard spinning such yarns of the shrines they had visited, you could tell by the way they talked that their tongues were more tuned to lying than telling the truth, no matter what tale they told.[11]

Indeed, a century earlier Berthold of Regensburg (1210–72) had noted in his *Two and Twenty Virtues* that experiences on pilgrimage had even become the subject of idle chatter in the church pews!

Other criticism was provoked by the increasing devotion paid to holy relics and religious imagery, so that there were those who felt that such objects constituted a distraction or deviation from the intended focus, Christ Himself. Writers and preachers feared that the excessive adoration bestowed on holy relics fostered idolatory and superstition, especially as many such relics could not be authenticated. Thomas More wrote his *Dyalogue on the Adoracion of Images* in order to express his own misgivings. St Bernard of Clairvaux (1090–1153), John Wycliffe, the fourteenth-century leader of the Lollards, and Desiderius Erasmus (*c.* 1466–1536) were other prominent men of God who voiced their anxieties at the mystique and adoration attached to saints and their relics:

> they view and venerate their bones, covered with silks and gold . . . and one seldom hears that any amendment of life results . . . but here in the sacrament of the Altar, You are wholly present my God.[12]

By the fourteenth century, John Wycliffe had also taken a vociferous stand against the power of the Pope to proclaim a man a saint, discounting Becket as a holy martyr and denying that there was any virtue in so-called miracle-working relics. After his death in 1384 his Lollard followers continued to uphold and spread his heretical views well into the fifteenth century. In his writings on images and pilgrimage he argued that those visiting holy shrines had come to attach all 'marvellous and precious works' to images of God and the holy family, these having been man-made to the design of the pilgrim's common imagination, 'the Father as an old man, and the Son as a young man on a cross'.[13]

The Lollards were particularly sceptical about the professed pious intent of monastic clergy in exhibiting their holy relics for the good of the pilgrim's soul and they criticised their devious behaviour as an attempt to draw in pilgrims for their own profit. In a study of mixed Lollard and non-Lollard relationships, Shannon McSheffrey cites examples of married couples where the Lollard husband attempted to discourage his wife from going on pilgrimage, reasoning thus – to the wife who wishes to visit a shrine of Our Lady, that the Virgin is not there, she is in Heaven; to another that she should bestow the expense of a pilgrimage on the poor and needy instead, not upon graven images; and to another wife, the counsel that priests only encourage pilgrimage for their own benefit, not for that of the pilgrim.[14]

The Lollards consistently argued against the excessive worship of relics, stating that the figure of God Himself came to be overlooked in the mist of such misplaced infatuation with relics and holy objects. Later, such criticism was reflected in the admonitions of John Calvin (1509–64): 'When Christ ought to have been sought in his word, sacraments and spiritual influences, the world, after its wont, clung to his garments, vests and swaddling clothes.'[15]

There was certainly some truth in the assertion of the over-whelming power that relics had assumed over the medieval mind. With their massive influx into Europe in the seventh century and their continued and ever increasing popularity thereafter came the contrivance of fake or invented relics, as well as the theft of relics from one religious house in order to establish a pilgrim following and income at another. The leaders of religious houses were quick to recognise the drawing power and compelling mysticism of such objects for the medieval pilgrim and so went to some effort to ensure that they were appropriately 'dressed up' in gold and jewelled caskets or shrines, thus heightening their perceived supernatural and ethereal qualities. Some religious houses even set in train projects to expand the fabric of their buildings, as in the case of St Denis Abbey under Abbot Suger, in order to facilitate access for the pilgrim, and, no doubt, to allow many more to enter at a time.

Particularly sardonic in his approach to the proclaimed efficacy of holy relics was the humanist scholar Erasmus. Writing after his own visit to the shrine of Our Lady at Walsingham in 1512, he is not so easily drawn by the ambience of wonder and excitement as are his fellow pilgrims entering the building, stating simply that 'the church is graceful and elegant; but the Virgin does not occupy it'.[16] On beholding the phial purported to contain the Virgin's milk that constituted Walsingham's most precious holy relic, Erasmus described its contents as an unappealing congealed mess, like 'ground chalk, mixed with the white of egg'![17] Other relics that were the object both of intrigue and devotional attention for pilgrims would also fall into disrepute on the eve of the Reformation, such as the phial of holy blood exhibited at the Cistercian abbey of Hailes in Gloucestershire which came to be discounted as duck's blood, replaced by the monks each day.

Worse, because consciously dishonest, than the excessive or mis-placed adoration bestowed on holy relics was the greed and profit-eering of their guardians who benefited from the homage paid them. With the Protestant Reformation came much more vitriolic criticism of pilgrimages, the Protestant reformer Martin Luther following this line of thought in the sixteenth century, influenced by men such as John Wycliffe and John Huys. In criticising the avaricious greed of some within the Church he stated that every bishop sought to have a shrine in his own diocese in order to benefit from the generous incomes such pilgrimage shrines accrued:

> No bishop forbids and no preacher rebukes such a perverse practice [pilgrimage]. In fact, in the interests of their own covetousness, the clergy endorse such practices. Every day they think up more and more pilgrimages.[18]

There is, too, evidence that some religious houses went so far as to fake miracles to fool the expectant pilgrim into believing that they had witnessed a divine marvel, such as a statue of the Virgin that shed real tears. Those who sought to foster pilgrimage sites in their own diocese or parish were also held up for scrutiny:

> Some priest to bring up a pilgrimage in his parish, may devise some false fellow feigning himself to come and seek a saint in his

church and there suddenly say that he hath gooten his sight. Then ye shall have bells rung for a miracle, and the fond folk of the country soon made fools.[19]

There was an underlying sense that the practice of pilgrimage had become derailed to such an extent that the Church no longer had the authority to control the pilgrim's motivation, with many now lacking the pious incentive or devout heart originally prescribed as part of the rationale behind pilgrimage. As has been mentioned earlier, there were also those who, aside from using it for personal, pleasurable gain, were abusing its practice by using it as a cover for other, more underhand purposes, such as romantic trysts, escape from responsibility, from husbands or wives, while still enjoying the privileges afforded the pilgrim in the way of free accommodation and the receipt of alms and other charity.

A document of 1473 records how the healthy had come to feign sickness in order to go away on pilgrimage to a shrine under the guise of a journey for personal healing; how others pretended to be pilgrims when they were not, so lapsing into aimless wanderings, 'living idly', begging and upsetting the natural order of things, causing disquiet and threatening the very fabric of society by which 'many other inconveniences follow by occasion of the same, as murders, robberies, riots, mischievous to the disturbance of the people and contrary to the King's law and peace . . .'.[20]

In one such case of 1412, the shuttlemaker William Blakeney had pretended to be a hermit, announcing that he had made pilgrimages to Rome, Venice, Jerusalem and other shrines, whereby 'under colour of such falsehood he had received many good things from divers persons, to the defrauding, and in manifest deceit, of all the people'. When brought to justice at Guildhall, he admitted to having practised his deception for six years; the court judged that he should be consigned to the pillory for three market-days for one hour each day with a whetstone hung about his neck.[21]

During the dissolution of the monasteries under Henry VIII, of those that held relics and drew in considerable numbers of pilgrims – places the King had come to loathe and whose wealth he coveted – approximately 563 monasteries were dissolved and roughly 9,000 monks and nuns poorly pensioned off.

It seems that particular attention was paid to the destruction of those objects of devotion most venerated by women, such as those from the shrines dedicated to the ever-popular cult of the Virgin. This saw several statues of Our Lady ceremoniously burnt on a pyre in Chelsea in 1538, including those from Walsingham, Ipswich and Willesden: 'the name of religion is used as a cover for superstition, faithlessness, foolishness, and recklessness'.[22]

In his criticism of housewives undertaking pilgrimage, Thomas More had noted the number of women engaged on the seemingly trivial visiting of the housekeeper St Zita on account of lost keys. Aside from highlighting the differences between male and female perspectives and expectations of pilgrimage, his strictures also represented a concern for the deviation of women's attentions from their appropriate focus as well as the corrupting effect on their thoughts and beliefs.

Hence it came to pass that the sacred settings, revered objects and spiritual incentives for the pilgrimages of medieval men and women were stripped bare, burnt and taken away. The focus of their devotions, the religious imagery that adorned such shrines and in the holy objects that purported to bear testimony to the earthly existence of the saints they venerated were no longer to be viewed, at least in England.

The Reformation and dissolution of the monasteries represented a fundamental turning point in medieval religious practice and in that of pilgrimage. In England the foundation stones for the veneration of holy sites, images and relics had been laid by Gregory the Great when he sent Augustine on a divine mission to banish England's pagan beliefs and replace them with Christianity and its teachings. The marking out of holy locations such as those in the Holy Land under Constantine the Great was to act as a spur to the journeys of anticipatory souls from their homes to newly venerated locations that held out great promise for the sick, crippled, or childless pilgrim. With the growing audience for saints' legends and the dissemination of accounts of the holy miracles said to have occurred at such places, the popularity of pilgrimage grew. With it came an increased trade in holy relics which stimulated a more supernatural and ethereal resonance with the holy places, laying the basis for a profusion of newly attested miracles.

In a society that by its very nature bred insecurity and fear, the medieval mind was ripe to absorb and fully appreciate all that such locations and holy relics had to offer. Here were means by which the individual who undertook pilgrimage could get nearer to God or his chosen saint on a more personal level, through prayer at the place where they had lived, died or were buried, supported by the vestiges of their existence that seemed to offer a tangible and more concrete basis for belief.

Pilgrims could select for their destination the shrines of those saints who resonated most strongly with their own needs. With their very specific expectations and rigidly defined social orbit, women perhaps formed the most powerful and poignant of such affiliations. Today, pilgrimage continues to be a popular activity among men, women, the elderly and all strata of society. It is still employed to seek a cure for illness or disability as at Lourdes; to reconnect with biblical teachings, perhaps most powerfully at the sacred locations of the Holy Land; and by those who seek companionship, to satisfy their curiosity by visiting new places and, of course, by those of devotional heart.

The modern-day woman pilgrim's actions and incentives are no longer as delimited by the teachings of the Church as they once were, or as commonly curbed by societal restraints, although perhaps more than ever the restrictions of time, work or family commitments can play their part. Pilgrimage is no longer seen as an essential means for spiritual salvation and while, for example, pilgrims may still justifiably journey to the awe-inspiring Cathedral of St James at Santiago de Compostela for this purpose, they are equally to be found at the tomb of an inspirational figure, paying their respects at the war graves of Europe, meditating on a quiet hill-top or at any other location imbued with personal significance. For pilgrimage continues to represent an opportunity for comradeship, merriment and adventure, as well as a means for introspection, pious devotion and spiritual alignment.

Conclusion

Apparently gender neutral and endorsed as a spiritual act by the Church, the practice of pilgrimage by medieval women reveals how their sex faced certain perennial issues, some of which drove them to undertake such journeys. These issues were inevitably and inextricably linked to their roles as carers, mothers and women with domestic responsibilities. We have seen that women travelled on pilgrimage as expectant mothers, to petition for the safety and health of their families, on account of a deceased spouse, as well as to seek remedy for gender-specific illnesses. Some female pilgrims also embodied a desire to break free from the constraints of the rigid domestic regime to which they were normally subject and, in the same way as some of their male counterparts, used pilgrimage as a means to effect their escape.

Some accounts of medieval women pilgrims that survive from as early as the fourth century represent these women as among the most eager, ascetically pious and devoted pilgrims, some electing to become permanent residents in the holy places they visit, others choosing as a consequence of their experience to join nunneries or take up the anchoritic life, others still simply embarking on pilgrimage for the sole purpose of furthering their spiritual growth and drawing themselves closer to God.

Conclusion

It might be argued that women had the most to gain by going on pilgrimage, not only to experience the kind of travel so often denied them or limited by the nature of their everyday lives, but in their capacity as dutiful petitioners for the health and preservation of their kin. However, they might also have the most to lose, subject to the very same dangers and hazards as beset their male companions but with the prospect of those additional threats to their safety posed by their sex. Margery Kempe's constant fear that she might be robbed of her new-found chastity by one of her male pilgrim companions is of genuine concern to her, and not unjustified.

Women were also to suffer the most opposition to going on pilgrimage. By the fourteenth century they were being held up as examples of its less honourable aspects in efforts to discredit it. While lascivious or inappropriate conduct on pilgrimage occurred among both men and women, as the perceived weaker, more vulnerable sex, it was always women who attracted the greatest concern from the outset and who were later held to account when some of their number strayed from the intended spiritual path. However, despite such opposition, women played a profound part in the practice of pilgrimage: in fulfilment of their duty to husband and family; in enhancing the popularity of certain shrines and saints as donors and protectors; in the establishment of the popular cult of the Virgin; and as the pilgrims, anchoresses, visionaries and canonised figures who recorded their experiences in written or dictated accounts to serve as the inspiration for many more women pilgrims who followed them, to this very day. A fitting close to our study is provided by the words of Brother Felix Fabri on his first sighting of the Holy Land:

'Pilgrims, rise up and come on deck; behold, the land which you long to see is in sight!' On hearing this shout all hurriedly rushed forth from every corner of the galley, men and women, old and young, sick and well, and climbed aloft that they might behold the land for whose sake they had left their native country, and exposed themselves to many hardships and to the danger of death.[1]

Notes

Introduction

1. J. Sumption, *Pilgrimage: An Image of Medieval Religion*, Princeton, NJ, 1975, p. 263.

Chapter One

1. *The Paston Letters*, ed. Norman Davis, Oxford, 1963, p. 6.
2. See *The Ancrene Riwle*, trans. M.D. Salu, London, 1955 and *The Ancrene Wisse*, Corpus Christi College, Cambridge, 402, EETS 249, London, 1961.
3. Christine de Pisan, *The Treasure of the City of Ladies*, trans. Sarah Lawson, London, 1985, p. 168.
4. Diana Webb, *Pilgrims and Pilgrimage in the Medieval West*, London, 1999, p. 168.
5. Diana Webb, 'Women Pilgrims of the Middle Ages', *History Today* 48, no. 7 (July 1998), 20–6.
6. Webb, *Pilgrims and Pilgrimage*, p. 95.
7. Diana Webb, *Medieval European Pilgrimage*, London, 2002.
8. See R.C. Finucane, *The Rescue of the Innocents: Endangered Children in Medieval Miracles* (London, 1997) for a full study of this particular subject.
9. Henry Harrod, 'Extracts From Early Wills in the Norwich Registers', *Norfolk Archaeology* 4 (1855), pp. 317–39.
10. Pietro Azario, 'Liber Gestorum in Lombardia', Rerum Italicurum Scriptores, 16, pp. 93–4.
11. *The Book of Wanderings of Brother Felix Fabri*, trans. Aubrey Stewart, Palestine Pilgrims' Text Society, London, 1887–97, Vol. 2, part 1, p. 293.

Notes

Chapter Two

1. John Wilkinson, *Egeria's Travels*, London, 1971.
2. Diana Webb, *Pilgrims and Pilgrimage in the Medieval West*, London, 1999, p. 246.
3. *The Travels of Sir John Mandeville*, trans. C.W.R.D. Moseley, London, 1983, p. 78.
4. Wilkinson, *Egeria's Travels*, p. 137.
5. *The Travels of Sir John Mandeville*, trans. Moseley, p. 77.
6. Wilkinson, *Egeria's Travels*, pp. 176–7.
7. *Ibid.*, p. 178.
8. *Ibid.*, pp. 122–3.
9. J. Sumption, *Pilgrimage*, London, 2002, p. 91.
10. *The Letter of Paula and Eustochium to Marcella about the Holy Places (365AD)*, trans. Aubrey Stewart, Palestine Pilgrims' Text Society, London, 1896.
11. J. Stopford, *Pilgrimage Explored*, York, 1999, p. 43.
12. Translated from *Les revelations celestes de Sainte Brigitte de Suede*, Librairie catholique Deperisse frères, Paris and Lyon, 1859.
13. St Bridget's *Liber Celestis Revelaciones*, 1:10.
14. *Saint Bride and Her Book. Birgitta of Sweden's Revelations*, trans. from Middle English by Julia Bolton Holloway, Focus Texts, MA, 1992.

Chapter Three

1. Christine de Pisan, *The Treasure of the City of Ladies*, trans. Sarah Lawson, London, 1985.
2. Diana Webb, *Pilgrims and Pilgrimage in the Medieval West*, London, 1999, p. 157.
3. *Ibid.*, p. 132.
4. *Book of Wanderings of Brother Felix Fabri*, trans. Aubrey Stewart, Palestine Pilgrims' Text Society, London, 1887–97, ch. 3.
5. *Ibid.*
6. *The Book of Margery Kempe*, trans. B.A. Windeatt, London, 1985, p. 97.
7. J. Wilkinson, *Egeria's Travels*, London, 1971, p. 177.
8. *Book of Wanderings of Brother Felix Fabri*, p. 11.
9. *Ibid.*
10. *Ibid.*
11. J. Crow (ed.), *Les Quinze Joies de Mariage*, Oxford, 1969, p. 58.
12. Geoffrey Chaucer, *General Prologue to the Canterbury Tales*, ed. James Winny, Cambridge, 1989, ll. 689–91.
13. T. Wright (ed.), *The Book of the Knight of La Tour-Landry*, Early English Text Society, o.s. 33, London, 1868, rev. edn 1906.

14. *Ibid.*
15. *Book of Wanderings of Brother Felix Fabri*, p. 19.
16. Wilkinson, *Egeria's Travels*, Oxford, 1999, pp. 93–4.

Chapter Four

1. *The Book of Margery Kempe*, trans. B.A. Windeatt, London, 1985, ch. 28, p. 103.
2. *Ibid.*, p. 42.
3. *Ibid.*, p. 124.
4. *Ibid.*, p. 101.
5. *Ibid.*, p. 285.
6. William Wey, *Itineraries to Jerusalem, 1458*, Roxburghe Club, London, 1857, p. 6.
7. *The Book of Margery Kempe*, p. 103.
8. *Ibid.*, p. 104.
9. *Ibid.*, p. 110.
10. *Ibid.*, p. 123.

Chapter Five

1. Geoffrey Chaucer, *General Prologue to the Canterbury Tales*, ed. James Winny, Cambridge, 1989, ll. 469–70.
2. Chaucer, *The Wife of Bath's Prologue and Tale*, ed. Winny, Cambridge, 1994, ll. 409–12.
3. *Ibid.*, ll. 651–3; from Ecclesiastes 25:25.
4. *The Wife of Bath's Prologue and Tale*, ll. 657–8.
5. *Ibid.*, ll. 925–8.
6. *Ibid.*, l. 950.
7. Chaucer, *General Prologue to the Canterbury Tales*, ll. 160–3, 1038–40.
8. Albert B. Friedman, 'The Prioress's Tale and Chaucer's Anti-Semitism' in *Chaucer Reviews*, 9, 1974, 118–29.
9. Chaucer, *General Prologue to the Canterbury Tales*, ll. 139–40.
10. *Ibid.*, ll. 124–6.
11. John Matthews Manly, *Some New Light on Chaucer: Lectures Delivered at the Lowell Institute, Gloucester*, New York, 1926, pp. 213–15.
12. Caesarius, *The Rule for Nuns*, trans. Mother Maria Caritas McCarthy, Catholic University of America Press, Washington, 1960, ch. 39.
13. A letter of Pope Gregory X (1271–6) incorporated material from earlier letters of Innocent III (1198–1216) and Innocent IV (1243–54) exposing the blood libel: Letter printed in B. Tierney, *Middle Ages: Sources of Medieval History*, Vol. 1, pp. 259–60, Berkshire, 1992.

Chapter Six

1. Geoffrey Chaucer, *General Prologue to the Canterbury Tales*, ed. James Winny, Cambridge, 1989, ll. 118–20.
2. Diana Webb, *Pilgrims and Pilgrimage in the Medieval West*, London, 1999, p. 14.
3. *Ibid.*, p. 31.
4. Chaucer, *General Prologue to the Canterbury Tales*, ll. 180–1.
5. Webb, *Pilgrims and Pilgrimage in the Medieval West*, p. 42.
6. *The Book of Wanderings of Brother Felix Fabri*, trans. Aubrey Stewart, Palestine Pilgrims' Text Society, London, 1887–97, Vol. 2, pt 1, p. 293.
7. Pope Innocent III to two Spanish bishops. Epistle 187, 11 December 1210, PL 216: 356. See *Decretals of Gregory IX*, Corpus Juris Canonici Lib. V, tit. 38, *De Poenitent*, ch. 10, *Nova*, ed. J. Friedberg Leipzig, Bernhard, Tauchmitz, 1928, Vol. 2 coll. 886–7.
8. Diana Webb, *Medieval European Pilgrimage*, New York, 2002.
9. Webb, *Pilgrims and Pilgrimage in the Medieval West*, p. 250.
10. *Ibid.*, p. 79.
11. *Ibid.*, p. 119.
12. A. Kendall, *Medieval Pilgrims*, London, 1986, p. 21.
13. Webb, *Pilgrims and Pilgrimage in the Medieval West*, p. 249.
14. *The Book of Wanderings of Brother Felix Fabri*.
15. *Ibid.*
16. Elizabeth M. Makowski, *Canon Law and Cloistered Women: Pericoloso and its Commentators 1298–1545*, Washington, DC, 1998, p. 30.
17. *The Letters of Abelard and Heloise*, ed. and trans. B. Radice, Epistle 7.
18. Makowski, *Canon Law and Cloistered Women*, p. 149.
19. Chaucer, *The Man of Law's Tale*, ll. 31–4.
20. *The Book of Margery Kempe*, trans. B.A. Windeatt, London, 1985, ch. 28, p. 46.
21. *Ibid.*, p. 82.
22. Desiderius Erasmus, *Pilgrimages to Saint Mary of Walsingham and Saint Thomas of Canterbury*, trans. J.G. Nichols, London, 1849, p. 13.

Chapter Seven

1. *The Paston Letters*, ed. Norman Davis, Oxford, 1963, Letter from John Paston II to John Paston III, 15 September, 1471.
2. Christine de Pisan, *The Treasure of the City of Ladies*, trans. Sarah Lawson, London, 1985.
3. C.G. Coulton (ed.), *Life in the Middle Ages*, New York, *c.* 1910, Vol. 1, pp. 1–7.
4. Diana Webb, *Medieval European Pilgrimage*, New York, 2002.

5. Jennifer C. Ward, *Women of the English Nobility and Gentry, 1066–1500*, London, 1995, p. 219.
6. Diana Webb, *Pilgrims and Pilgrimage in the Medieval West*, London, 1999, pp. 104–5.
7. S. Signe Morrison, *Women Pilgrims in Late Medieval Engand: Private Piety as Public Performance*, London, 2000, p. 48.
8. Ward, *Women of the English Nobility and Gentry*, p. 207.
9. *The Treasure of the City of Ladies*, trans. Lawson, p. 84.
10. T. Wright (ed.), *The Book of the Knight of La Tour-Landry*, Early English Text Society, o.s. 32, London, 2000.
11. Webb, *Pilgrims and Pilgrimage in the Medieval West*, p. 183.
12. J. Sumption, *Pilgrimage: An Image of Medieval Religion*, Princeton, NJ, 1975, p. 247.
13. *Ibid.*
14. Edward became King of England the following year when news reached the Holy Land that King Henry III had died on 16 November 1272.
15. Matthew Paris, *La Estorie de Seint Aedward le rei*, trans. Katherine Young Wallace, ANTS 41, Anglo-Norman Text Society, London, 1983
16. See Nicholas Harris, *Privy Purse Expenses of Elizabeth of York: Wardrobe Accounts of Edward IV*, New York, 1972.
17. See Ward, *Women of the English Nobility and Gentry*, for more details of the Privy Purse expenses of Elizabeth de Burgh.

Chapter Eight

1. Geoffrey Chaucer, *General Prologue to the Canterbury Tales*, ed. James Winny, Cambridge, 1989, ll. 689–91.
2. R.C. Finucane, *Miracles and Pilgrims: Popular Beliefs in Medieval England*, New York, 1977, p. 127.
3. H. Deeming, 'The Songs of St Godric: A Neglected Context', *Music and Letters* 86, no. 2 (2005), pp. 169–85.
4. Finucane, *Miracles and Pilgrims*, p. 169.
5. Geoffrey de La Tour-Landry, *The Booke of Thenseygnementes and Techynge that the Knyght of the Tower made to his Doughters*, London, G. Newnes, 1902.
6. For more information on the Dissolution and the fate of England's cathedrals see Eamon Duffy, *The Stripping of the Altars*, Yale, 1992 and D.H. Turner, 'The Customary of the Shrine of St Thomas Becket', *Canterbury Chronicle*, 70, 1976.
7. J. Sumption, *Pilgrimage: An Image of Medieval Religion*, Princeton, NJ, 1975, p. 153.
8. John Calvin, *An Admonition Concerning Relics*, Buckinghamshire, 1995, p. 5.
9. Sumption, *Pilgrimage*, p. 31.

10. *The Autobiography of Guibert, Abbot of Nogent-sous-Couc'y*, trans. C.C. Swinton Bland, London and New York, 1925, ch. 12.
11. *Ibid.*
12. Sumption, *Pilgrimage*, p. 49.
13. *Ibid.*, p. 51.
14. *Ibid.*, p. 75.
15. Desiderius Erasmus, *Pilgrimages to Saint Mary of Walsingham and Saint Thomas of Canterbury*, trans. J.G. Nichols, London, 1875, p. 8.
16. John Wilkinson, *Egeria's Travels*, London, 1971, pp. 160–1.
17. *The Travels of Sir John Mandeville*, trans. C.W.R.D. Moseley, Harmondsworth, 1983, p. 70.
18. J. Stopford, *Pilgrimage Explored*, York, 1991, pp. 148–9.
19. Version of a prayer recited to request St Catherine's help; S. Dewar 'St Catherine of Alexandria and her cult at Abbotsbury', *Proceedings of the Dorset Natural History and Archaeological Society* 90 (1969), pp. 261–3.
20. T. Nyberg, *Birgitta hendes værk og hendes klostre i Norden* ('Birgitta, her Works, and her Five Abbeys in the Nordic Countries'), Odense, Denmark, 1991, p. 85.
21. Johannes Jorgensen, *Saint Bridget of Sweden*, 2 vols, Longman, Green, 1954.
22. Later accounts note these relics as *furta sacra*, stolen relics, from Provence.
23. Calendars of Patent Rolls, Ed. II 1, p. 76, cited in Diana Webb, *Pilgrims and Pilgrimage in the Medieval West*, London, 1999, p. 171.

Chapter Nine

1. *The Romance of Reynard the Fox*, trans. D.D.R. Owen, Oxford, 1994, p. 142.
2. See Chapter 8 for more on Vèzelay.
3. For more information on the routes concerned and those excursions and halts popular with pilgrims, see S. Hopper, *To Be a Pilgrim: The Medieval Pilgrimage Experience*, Stroud, 2002.
4. W. Stubbs, *Seventeen Lectures*, Oxford, 1886, VI, p. 128.
5. William Wey, *Itineraries to Jerusalem, 1458*, Roxburghe Club, London, 1857, p. 4.
6. F.J. Furnivall and W.G. Stone (eds), *The Tale of Beryn*, New York, 1981.
7. Theoderich, *Guide to the Holy Land*, trans. A. Stewart, New York, 1986, part 1, XIII, p. 22.
8. With thanks to the Eastbridge Hospital, Canterbury. For pilgrims at Canterbury who arrived by sea, there was another hospital, affiliated to St John, at the port of Sandwich and founded at 1280.
9. *Cartulaire général de l'Ordre des Hospitaliers de S. Jean de Jerusalem, 1100–1310*, ed. J. Delaville Le Roulx, 4 vols, Vol. 1, no. 627, Paris, 1894–1906, pp. 425–9.

Notes

10. Julie Ann Smith, 'Sacred Journeying: Women's Correspondence and Pilgrimage in the Fourth and Eighth Centuries', in J. Stopford, *Pilgrimage Explored*, York, 1999, p. 45.
11. *The Book of Wanderings of Brother Felix Fabri*, trans. Stewart, Palestine Pilgrims' Text Society, London, 1887–97, Vol. 2, pt 1, pp. 280–1.
12. *Ibid.*
13. Diana Webb, *Pilgrims and Pilgrimage in the Medieval West*, London, 1999, p. 33.
14. *Ibid.*, p. 248.
15. *Ibid.*, p. 102.
16. *Ibid.*, pp. 200–1.
17. *Ibid.*, Vol. 2, pt 2, p. 318.
18. Diana Webb, *Pilgrims and Pilgrimage in the Medieval West*, London, 1999,p. 103.
19. *Ibid.*, p. 178.
20. E.V. Utterson, *Early Popular Poetry*, Vol. 1, London, 1817.

Chapter Ten

1. Pietro Azario, 'Liber Gestorum Lombardia', Rerum Italicarum Scriptores 16. iv, pp. 93–4.
2. S. Signe Morrison, *Women Pilgrims in Late Medieval England: Private Piety as Public Performance*, London, 2000, p. 59.
3. *Statuti di Perugia dell'Anno MCCCXLIII*, ed. G. degli Azzi, 2 vols, Loescher Editore, Rome, 1913, pp. 120–1.
4. Diana Webb, *Pilgrims and Pilgrimage in the Medieval West*, London, 1999, p. 210.
5. Signe Morrison, *Women Pilgrims in Late Medieval Engand*, p. 57.
6. *The Book of Wanderings of Brother Felix Fabri*, trans. Aubrey Stewart, Palestine Pilgrims' Text Society, London, 1887–97.
7. *Ibid.*
8. Signe Morrison, *Women Pilgrims in Late Medieval England*, p. 60.
9. *The Greenlanders' Saga*, trans. George Johnston, Oberon Press, Ottawa, 1976.
10. *The Book of Wanderings of Brother Felix Fabri*, trans. Stewart, Vol. 2, pt 1, p. 32.
11. William Wey, *Itineraries to Jerusalem, 1458*, 1857, Roxburghe Club, London, p. 7.
12. *The Book of Margery Kempe*, trans. B.A. Windeatt, London, 1985, p. 110.
13. John Wilkinson, *Egeria's Travels*, London, 1971, 3.1–3.2, p. 93.
14. Wey, *Itineraries to Jerusalem*, p. 6.
15. *Ibid.*, p. 7.
16. *Abbot Suger on the Abbey Church of St Denis and its Art Treasures*, Princeton, NJ, 1946, pp. 87–93.
17. J. Sumption, *Pilgrimage*, London, 2002, p. 263.
18. Theoderich, *Guide to the Holy Land*, New York, 1986, part I, XII, p. 19.

19. Giovanni Villani, *Nuova Cronica*, ed. G. Porta, Florence, 1990–1, Vol. 2, pp. 37–8; Webb, *Pilgrims and Pilgrimage in the Medieval West*, p. 117.

20. *Chronicon Astense: Memoriale Giuliemi Venturae civis Astensis*, in L.A. Muratori, Rerum Italicarum Scriptores, 1300, 11, cols 191–2, cited in Webb, *Pilgrims and Pilgrimage in the Medieval West*, p. 118.

21. J. Sumption, *Pilgrimage: An Image of Medieval Religion*, Princeton, NJ, 1975, p. 263.

22. *Diario della Città di Roma di Stefano Infessura, Fonto della Storia d'Italia 5*, pp. 48–9, cited in Webb, *Pilgrims and Pilgrimage in the Medieval West*, pp. 121–2.

23. *The Book of Margery Kempe*, trans. B.A. Windeatt, p. 281.

24. R.B. Dobson, *The Peasants Revolt of 1381*, London, 1970, p. 133, and 'Froissart – Chronicles', trans. Geoffrey Brereton, Penguin, Harmondsworth, 2004.

Chapter Eleven

1. *The Book of Wanderings of Brother Felix Fabri*, trans. Aubrey Stewart, Palestine Pilgrims' Text Society, London, 1887–97, Vol. 1, pt 2, ch. 4.

2. *The Book of Margery Kempe*, trans. B.A. Windeatt, London, 1985, p. 107.

3. *The Book of Wanderings of Brother Felix Fabri*, trans. Stewart, ch. 4.

4. William Wey, *Itineraries to Jerusalem, 1458*, Roxburghe Club, London, 1857, p. 14.

5. *The Travels of Sir John Mandeville*, trans. C.W.R.D. Moseley, London, 1983, p. 91

6. *The Book of Margery Kempe*, Harmondsworth, 1994, ch. 26, p. 96.

7. Due to Henry V's requisitioning of the ships for his expedition to France.

8. *The Book of Margery Kempe*, Harmondsworth, 1994, ch. 26, p. 178.

9. The guardians of St Cuthbert's tomb had reported the continuing growth of the corpse's beard and nails, requiring their regular trimming and upkeep.

10. J. Sumption, *Pilgrimage: An Image of Medieval Religion*, Princeton, NJ, 1975, p. 263.

11. P. Geary, *Furta Sacra*, Princeton, NJ, 1991, p. 17.

12. Sumption, *Pilgrimage*, p. 24

13. *Quinze Joies de Mariage*, J. Rychner (ed.), Paris, 1967.

14. *The Book of Margery Kempe*, Harmondsworth, 1994, ch. 26, p. 113.

15. Diana Webb, *Pilgrims and Pilgrimage in the Medieval West*, London, 1999, p. 248.

16. *Julian of Norwich, Revelations of Divine Love*, Harmondsworth, 1966, p. 76.

17. Sumption, *Pilgrimage*, p. 91

18. See R.C. Finucane, *The Rescue of the Innocents: Endangered Children in Medieval Miracles*, London, 1997.

19. For an assessment of all the stained glass at Canterbury Cathedral, see M.A. Michael, *Stained Glass of Canterbury Cathedral*, London, 2004.

20. The 'Miracle Windows', Trinity Chapel, Canterbury Cathedral, Window n. IV, 49, 50.

Notes

Chapter Twelve

1. Christine de Pisan, *The Treasure of the City of Ladies*, trans. Sarah Lawson, London, 1985.
2. *Ibid.*, p. 168.
3. *Ibid.*
4. Geoffrey Chaucer, *General Prologue to the Canterbury Tales*, ed. James Winny, Cambridge, 1989, l. 13.
5. Thomas à Kempis, *The Imitation of Christ*, trans. Leo Sherley-Price, Harmondsworth, 1984, p. 186.
6. T. Wright (ed.), *The Book of the Knight of La Tour-Landry*, Early English Text Society, o.s. 33, London, 1868, rev. edn 1906, ch. 34.
7. *Ibid.*
8. *Ibid.*, pp. 47–51.
9. *The Book of Wanderings of Brother Felix Fabri*, trans. Aubrey Stewart, Palestine Pilgrims' Text Society, London, 1887–97, Vol. 1.
10. Desiderius Erasmus, *Pilgrimages to Saint Mary of Walsingham and Saint Thomas of Canterbury*, trans. J.G. Nichols, London, 1849.
11. William Langland, *Piers the Plowman*, trans. J.F. Goodridge, London, 1996, p. 26.
12. Thomas à Kempis, *Imitation of Christ*, trans. Leo Sherley-Price, p. 186.
13. A. Hudson, *English Wycliffite Writings*, Cambridge, 1981, ch. 12, p. 16, ll. 6–7.
14. S. McSheffrey, *Gender and Heresy: Women and Men in Lollard Communities*, Philadelphia, PA, 1995, p. 94.
15. John Calvin, *An Admonition Concerning Relics*, Buckinghamshire, 1995, p. 2.
16. Erasmus, *Pilgrimages to Saint Mary of Walsingham and Saint Thomas of Canterbury*, p. 13.
17. *Ibid.*, p. 23.
18. Helmut T. Lehmann and James Atkinson (eds), *Luther's Works*, Philadelphia, PA, 1966, 44.86.
19. J. Sumption, *Pilgrimage: An Image of Medieval Religion*, Princeton, NJ, 1975, p. 55.
20. Diana Webb, *Pilgrims and Pilgrimage in the Medieval West*, London, 1999, p. 211.
21. H.T. Riley, *Memorials of London and London Life, in the XIIIth, XIVth and XVth Centuries, A.D. 1276–1419*, London, 1868.
22. Desiderius Erasmus, *Colloquies*, trans. C.R. Thompson, University of Chicago Press, 1965, p. 626.

Conclusion

1. *The Book of Wanderings of Brother Felix Fabri*, trans. Aubrey Stewart, Palestine Pilgrims' Text Society, London, 1887–97, ch. 4.

Bibliography

Primary Sources

Alighieri, Dante, *La Vita Nuova*, trans. Barbara Reynolds, Penguin,
  Harmondsworth, 1969

Ancrene Wisse, Corpus Christi College, Cambridge, 402, Early English Texts
  Society 249, London, 1961

Bede, *History of the English Church and People*, trans. L. Sherley-Price and R.E.
  Latham, London, 1975

Bernard the Wise, *The Itinerary of Bernard the Wise (AD 870)*, trans. J.H. Bernard,
  London, 1893

Book of Margery Kempe, The, trans. B.A. Windeatt, London, 1985

Book of Wanderings of Brother Felix Fabri, The, trans. Aubrey Stewart, Palestine
  Pilgrims' Text Society, London, 1887–97

Caesarius, *The Rule for Nuns*, trans. Mother Maria Caritas McCarthy, Catholic
  University of America Press, Washington, 1960

Calvin, John, *An Admonition Concerning Relics*, John Metcalfe Publishing Trust,
  Buckinghamshire, 1995

Capgrave, John, *Ye Solace of Pilgrimes*, eds C.A. Mills and H.M. Bannister,
  Oxford, 1911

Chaucer, Geoffrey, *General Prologue to the Canterbury Tales*, ed. James Winny,
  Cambridge, 1989

——, *The Prioress's Prologue and Tale*, ed. James Winny, Cambridge, 1975

——, *The Wife of Bath's Prologue and Tale*, ed. James Winny, Cambridge, 1994

Christine de Pisan, *The Treasure of the City of Ladies*, trans. Sarah Lawson,
  Penguin, Harmondsworth, 1985

Chronicon Adae de Usk, 1377–1421, trans. C. Given-Wilson, Oxford, 1997

Crow, J. (ed.), *Les Quinze Joies de Mariage*, Oxford, 1969

Bibliography

D'Evelyn, C. (ed.), *Peter Idley's 'Instructions To His Son'*, Boston, 1935

Egeria: Diary of a Pilgrimage, trans. G.E. Gingras, 1970

Egeria's Travels in the Holy Land, trans. J. Wilkinson, Warminster, 1981

English Wycliffite Writings, intro. Anne Hudson, ch. 16: 'Images and Pilgrimages', Cambridge, 1978

Erasmus, Desiderius, *Pilgrimages to Saint Mary of Walsingham and Saint Thomas of Canterbury*, trans. J.G. Nichols, London, 1875

——, *Colloquies*, trans. C.R. Thompson, University of Chicago Press, 1965

Gervase, *Of the Burning and Repair of the Church of Canterbury in the Year 1174*, ed. Charles Cotton, Friends of Canterbury Cathedral, 1930

Gordon Duff, E. (ed.), *Information for Pilgrims unto the Holy Land*, London, 1893. (Reproduction of book printed by Wynken de Worde in 1498, 1515 and 1524 based on information from William Wey)

Greenlanders' Saga, The, trans. George Johnston, Oberon Press, Ottawa, 1976

Hadewijch, *The Complete Works*, trans. C. Hart, New York, 1980

Harff, Arnold von, *The Pilgrimage of Arnold Von Harff, Knight*, trans. from the German and ed. with notes and intro. by Malcolm Letts, F.S.A. Nendeln/Liechtenstein, Kraus Reprint, 1967

Josephus, *The Complete Works*, trans. William Whiston, Nashville, TN, 1998

Langland, William, *Piers the Ploughman*, trans. J.F. Goodridge, London, 1966

Letter of Paula and Eustochium to Marcella about the Holy Places (365AD), The, trans. Aubrey Stewart, Palestine Pilgrims' Text Society, London, 1896

Letters of Abelard and Heloise, The, ed. and trans. B. Radice, London, 1974

Master Gregorius, *Narracio de Mirabilibus Urbis Romae*, trans. John Osborne, Pontifical Institute of Medieval Studies, Ontario, 1987

Memorials of Saint Dunstan, Rolls Series 63, pp. 391–5 (for Sigeric's account)

Paston Letters, The, ed. Norman Davis, Oxford, 1963

Quinze Joies de Mariage, Les, ed. J. Rychner, Paris, 1967

Revelations celestes de Sainte Brigitte de Suede, Les, trans. Librairie catholique deperisse frères, Paris/Lyon, 1859

Romance of Reynard the Fox, The, trans. D.D.R. Owen, Oxford, 1994

Song of Roland, The, trans. Dorothy Sayers, Harmondsworth, 1971

Tale of Beryn, The, eds F.J. Furnivall and W.G. Stone, New York, 1981

Theoderich, *Guide to the Holy Land*, trans. A. Stewart, New York, 1986

Theodosius, *On the Topography of the Holy Land*, trans. J.H. Bernard, London, 1893

Thomas à Kempis, *The Imitation of Christ*, trans. Leo Sherley-Price, Penguin, Harmondsworth, 1984

Travels of Sir John Mandeville, The, trans. C.W.R.D. Moseley, 1987

Villani, Giovanni, *Nuova Cronica*, ed. G. Porta, 3 vols, Florence, 1990–1

Wey, William, *Itineraries to Jerusalem, 1458*, Roxburghe Club, 1857

Whittock, M. (ed.), *The Pastons in Medieval Britain*, Oxford, 1993

Bibliography

Wright, T. (ed.), *The Book of the Knight of La Tour-Landry*, Early English Text
  Society, London, 1969, rev. ed 1906, O.S. 33, 1868, 1906

Secondary Sources

Adair, J. and Chèze-Brown, P., *The Pilgrim's Way*, London, 1978

Alexander, J. and Binski, P., *Age of Chivalry – Art in Plantagenet England
  1200–1400*, London, 1987

Alexander, P., *The Life and Letters of Paul*, Berkhampstead, 1984

Biddle, M., *Tomb of Christ*, Stroud, 1999

Brereton, G.E. and Ferrier, J.M., *Le Ménagier de Paris*, Oxford, 1981

Brodrick, J., *Saint Ignatius Loyola, The Pilgrim Years*, London, 1956

Brown, P.R.L., *Relics and Social Status in the Age of Gregory of Tours*, Reading,
  1977

Bull, M. (trans.), *The Miracles of Our Lady of Rocamadour*, Woodbridge, 1999

Butler, H. (ed.), *The Chronicle of Jocelin of Brakeland*, London, 1949

Coelho, Paulo, *The Pilgrimage*, London, 1997

Coulton, G.G., *Medieval Panorama*, Cambridge, 1938

—— (ed.), *Life in the Middle Ages*, Vol. 10, New York, *c.* 1910

Darlington, R.R. (ed.), *Vita Wulfstani of William of Malmesbury*, London, 1928

Davidson, Linda Kay and Dunn-Wood, Maryjane, *Pilgrimage in the Middle Ages: A
  Research Guide*, New York, 1993

Deeming, H., 'The Songs of St Godric: A Neglected Context', *Music & Letters*, Vol.
  86, no. 2, Oxford University Press, 2005, 169–85

Dewar, S., 'St Catherine of Alexandria and her Cult at Abbotsbury', *Proceedings of
  the Dorset Natural History and Archaeological Society* 90, 1969

Elphinstone, M., *The Sea Road*, Edinburgh, 2001

Finucane, R.C., *Miracles and Pilgrims: Popular Beliefs in Medieval England*, New
  York, 1977

——, *The Rescue of the Innocents: Endangered Children in Medieval Miracles*,
  London, 1997

Geary, Patrick J., *Furta Sacra: Theft of Relics in the Central Middle Ages*, Princeton,
  NJ, 1978

Hall, D.J., *English Medieval Pilgrimage*, London, 1965

Heath, Sidney, *Pilgrim Life in the Middle Ages*, London, 1911

Hibbert, Christopher, *Rome, The Biography of a City*, New York, 1985

Jusserand, J.J., *English Wayfaring Life in the Middle Ages*, London, 1950

Kendall, Alan, *Medieval Pilgrims*, London, 1986

King, G.G., *The Way of St James*, New York and London, 1920

Lubin, L., *The Worcester Pilgrim*, Worcester, 1990

MacCulloch, J.A., *Medieval Faith and Fable*, London, 1932

McSheffery, S., *Gender and Heresy: Women and Men in Lollard Communities*,
  Philadelphia, PA, 1995

Bibliography

Makowski, Elizabeth M., *Canon Law and Cloistered Women: Pericoloso and its Commentators 1298–1545*, Washington, DC, 1998

Mancinelli, Fabrizio, *The Catacombs of Rome: and the Origins of Christianity*, Florence, 1981

Manly, John Matthews, *Some New Light on Chaucer: Lectures Delivered at the Lowell Institute, Gloucester*, New York, 1926

Michael, M.A., *Stained Glass of Canterbury Cathedral*, London, 2004

Morton, H.V., *In Search of the Holy Land*, London, 1979

Nicolas, N.H., *Privy Purse Expenses of Elizabeth of York: Wardrobe Accounts of Edward IV*, New York, 1972

Noffke, S. (trans.), *Catherine of Siena, The Letters of Catherine of Siena 1–70*, Medieval and Renaissance Texts and Studies Series, Arizona Centre for Medieval and Renaissance Studies, 2000

Nyberg, T., *Birgitta hendes værk og hendes klostre i Norden* (Birgitta, her Works, and her Five Abbeys in the Nordic Countries), Odense, Denmark, 1991

Ohler, N., *The Medieval Traveller*, trans. C. Hillier, Woodbridge, 1989

Oursel, R., *Les Pelerins du Moyen Age*, Paris, 1963

Parks, G.B., *The English Traveller to Italy*, Rome, 1954

Peters, F.E., *Jerusalem: The Holy City in the Eyes of Chroniclers, Visitors, Pilgrims and Prophets from the Days of Abraham to the Beginnings of Modern Times*, Princeton, NJ, 1985

Power, E., *The Goodman of Paris*, trans. from *Le Ménagier de Paris*, London, 1928

Prescott, H.F.M., *Friar Felix at Large: A Fifteenth-Century Pilgrimage to the Holy Land*, New Haven, CN, 1950

——, *Jerusalem Journey: Pilgrimage to the Holy Land in the Fifteenth Century*, London, 1954

Reader, I. and Walter, T. (eds), *Pilgrimage in Popular Culture*, London, 1993

Riley, H.T., *Memorials of London and London Life, in the XIIIth, XIVth and XVth Centuries, AD. 1276–1419*, London, 1868

Robertson, J.C. (ed.), *Materials for the History of Thomas Becket*, 7 vols, London, 1875–85

Rychner, J., (ed.), *Quinze Joies de Mariage*, Paris, 1967

Salu, M.D. (trans.), *The Ancrene Riwle*, London, 1955

The Sarum Missal in English, London, 1968

Signe Morrison, S., *Women Pilgrims in Late Medieval England: Private Piety as Public Performance*, London, 2000

Spencer, B., *Pilgrim Souvenirs and Popular Badges*, London, 1998

Stopford, J. (ed.), *Pilgrimage Explored*, York, 1999

Stubbs, W., *Seventeen Lectures*, Oxford, 1886

Sumption, J., *Pilgrimage: An Image of Medieval Religion*, Faber & Faber, London, 1975

——, *Pilgrimage*, London, 2002

Bibliography

Swinton Bland, C.C. (trans.), *The Autobiography of Guibert, Abbot of Nogent-sous-Coucy*, London, 1925

Tate, B. and Tate, M., *The Pilgrim Route to Santiago*, Oxford, 1987

Thiede, C.P. and D'Ancona, M., *The Quest for the True Cross*, London, 2000

Toulmin Smith, J., *English Gilds*, Oxford, 1870

Turner, D.H., 'The Customary of the Shrine of St Thomas Becket', *Canterbury Cathedral Chronicle*, no. 70, 1976

Utterson, E.V., *Early Popular Poetry*, London, 1817

Vielliard, J. (trans.), *Le Guide du Pélerin de Saint Jacques de Compostelle*, Mâcon, 1950

Ward, Jennifer C., *English Noblewomen in the Later Middle Ages*, London, 1992

——, *Women of the English Nobility and Gentry, 1066–1500*, London, 1995

Webb, D., *Pilgrims and Pilgrimage in the Medieval West*, London, 1999

——, *Medieval European Pilgrimage*, New York, 2002

Wilkinson, J., *Egeria's Travels*, London, 1971

——, *Jerusalem Pilgrims before the Crusades*, Warminster, 1977

——, *Jerusalem Pilgrimage 1099–1185*, London, 1988

Wolters, C. (trans.), *Julian of Norwich, Revelations of Divine Love*, Harmondsworth, 1966

Woodruff, C.E., 'The Financial Aspect of the Shrine of St Thomas of Canterbury', *Archaeolgia Cantiana*, Vol. 44, 1932

Wright, T. (ed.), *The Book of the Knight of la Tour-Landry*, Early English Text Society, O.S. 33, 2000

Zacher, C.K., *Curiosity and Pilgrimage: The Literature of Fourteenth-century Discovery in England*, John Hopkins University Press, Baltimore, 1976

Index

Note: References to places in the index are restricted to pilgrimage sites and shrines. Page numbers in **bold** indicate chapters.